COLLEGE MAJORS THAT WORK

....

A Step-By-Step Guide to Choosing and Using Your College Major

FIRST EDITION

BY
MICHAEL P. VIOLLT

OCTAMERON
ASSOCIATES

Address correspondence to:
Octameron Associates
PO Box 2748
Alexandria, VA 22301
703. 836. 5480 (voice)
703. 836. 5650 (fax)

octameron@aol.com (e-mail)
www.octameron.com

ISBN 1-57509-100-3
PRINTED IN THE UNITED STATES OF AMERICA

TABLE OF CONTENTS

Section 2: What your Choice Means

Section 3: The Majors

INTRODUCTION

During the 2011-2012 school year, the average annual cost of tuition, fees, room and board at a four-year, public university will be around $16,950. At a private university, it will be about $3,780. Is that money you can afford to waste?

A student that selects her major before starting college and who stays with that major to graduation will save, on average, 33% of the total cost of her education.

This book will help you make the right major choice at the point where so many dreams go astray and so much money goes out the window – the selection of a college major. There is no question that the type of school you select and its reputation is very important. But, if you really want to know where most students go wrong, it is when they fail to give enough time and thought to what they want to study and the time it will take to earn a marketable degree.

What is a marketable degree? It is a degree that will qualify you for professional employment in your chosen field.

Most students should not start college until they have committed to a major. And by committed, I mean that she has analyzed her goals, really gone over her likes and dislikes, and talked to others about her choices and options. Students need to know what degrees they are qualified to pursue and to what careers each field of study typically leads.

Why? The days when students could take two to three years to declare a major are truly over. College is just too big of an investment. Students often take up to six years to earn a bachelor's degree. Multiply six years times today's annual tuition rate and you quickly see how big your investment will be. But college is an investment you need to make.

Even the one-time "train-on-the-job" careers in manufacturing and skilled trades now require that prospective employees have college coursework and continuing education to qualify for a job. People are no longer working themselves up from the factory floor to management positions. Those days are over and those jobs are gone.

Everyone is going back to school. It has become the only clear path to the American dream. At the same time, the cost of college has sky-rocketed.

That means you better have a very good idea of what you want from a college education *before* **you start college.**

This book will take you through the process. Keep a pencil nearby – you will be completing some surveys to help you refine your thinking on the subject. When you are done, you may be more certain than ever that your childhood dream of becoming a doctor or computer engineer was absolutely the right choice for you. If, however, you finish reading and realize your goals have changed, you might be a little worried. But take heart – it is much better to find out early so you can adjust your decision accordingly.

You are going to see plenty of references to the 10-Cluster System. This system was developed to sort majors into groups by students' skill sets, preferences, expectations, and aptitudes. If you have spent any time with your high school guidance counselor, you have probably heard about career groupings, but as you will see in Chapter 5 and in the back of the book, this system is based on college majors not career paths. It includes the most popular fields of study at most colleges in the country.

This book is divided into three sections.

Section One focuses on selecting a major

Section Two examines how your choice of major impacts other decisions

Section Three is devoted to information on the individual majors

By the way, do not be a college snob. You do not have to invest in an Ivy League degree and two to three years of graduate school to be a success in the world. One of the most exciting things about college options right now is that so many schools are offering certificate programs and associate degrees in fields that let you jump start your career and still finish your college education. Many students "road test" career choices with a two-year degree and enroll in four-year institutions or earn post-graduate degrees once their real-world, work experience has given them a better idea of the right career direction for them.

There is renewed interest in applied education – coursework that involves a lot of real-world experience, internship opportunities, and training from people currently working in the field. Every major should contain an applied education component because it is the best way for students to visualize themselves in potential careers. If students have to wait until their first day on the job to determine whether they have made the right choice of a major, they may become disappointed.

Here is another point to remember – chances are good you will be going back to school at least once during your lifetime. So keep this book handy– you might need it again in five to ten years.

SECTION 1

Selecting a Major

CHAPTER 1

■ ■ ■ ■ ■ ■ ■ ■ ■ ■ ■ ■ ■ ■ ■ ■ ■ ■ ■ ■

SELECTING A COLLEGE MAJOR IS IMPORTANT

Determining your college major is a huge turning point in your life. It is a selection process that will influence your future career options and your lifestyle alternatives. Yet, many students go about this process backwards. Most students select a college first and then choose a major. They select a college not for its strength in their intended field of study but for other reasons.

Some select a college for its location, or because their parents went there, or because it is one of the few they think they can afford. They think that selecting a major is not something they will have to do for two to three years after enrolling, so they put off thinking about it until later.

This approach creates problems. Failing to select a major, or selecting the wrong major, is one of the top reasons students fail to graduate from college. It is also the primary reason that it takes more than four years to finish for those who do graduate. Failing to select a major early can lead to the wrong college choice and is a waste of your time, enthusiasm, and money.

How Important is College?

Recent surveys show that holders of four-year baccalaureate degrees earn anywhere from $1 million to $2 million more on average during their working lives than those without college degrees – and the quality of their health, family life, and career satisfaction also tend to be better.

A survey released in 2003 by the *Chronicle of Higher Education* shows what students think are the most important outcomes of a college education:

- Prepares undergraduate students for a career
- Prepares students to be responsible citizens
- Provides education to adults so they can qualify for better jobs
- Prepares future leaders of our society

For at least half of all college students, higher education is about building a career path. Most other students recognize career development as an important goal of college. If the above list is representative of your feelings, then selecting a major is a critical decision for you.

What Selecting a Major Means

To an employer or a graduate school, your undergraduate major is your calling card. It reflects a tangible set of skills you are bringing to the world. It is why many schools still emphasize a "major and minor" system in which you select one primary field of study with a second, complementary field of study. This gives you a larger skill set to bring to the task, whether the task is a job or continuing your education on the graduate level.

Every student cannot walk into a college interview with a single, unwavering choice of what her major will be. College is a journey of discovery and people refocus their goals as they go through – that is actually very healthy. The focus of this book is to help you select a category – or cluster – of majors that best meet your talents and desires. If you have a cluster choice completed, you will have many of the same benefits of an individual major selection.

All majors have been broken down into a 10-Cluster System that you will hear much more about in Chapters 2 and 5. Think of clusters as college majors organized in specific groups because they require similar skills and are a good fit for certain types of people. Each cluster is also broken down by the specific amounts of education they require. In Chapter 9, you will see each of the majors sorted alphabetically, the cluster they fit into, symbols showing the expectations that each can meet for the average student, and web sites that can offer more insight into this career. This system can assist you in making your college education a good investment.

It is amazing when a prospective student says she wants to graduate from college and earn a big salary, buy a fancy car, and expensive home — yet pursues a career in a field like social work! There is no question that social work is a great and rewarding career. It meets many students' expectations but it does not typically pay a big salary. It is important that students explore their expectations and have a realistic idea about what lifestyle they want before they decide on a specific field of study.

Education is not just about the money you will earn, but it does make sense to start thinking in realistic terms about your career and lifestyle priorities before you get to college, no matter where you finally decide to go to school. This book will help you match your goals and expectations with the right major for you—the selection of the right college will then become much easier.

Degree	Average Offer (Fall 2003)	Percent Change (From 2002)
Accounting	$42,045	+4.4%
Business Administration	37,368	+6.1
Chemical Engineering	52,563	+2.5
Civil Engineering	41,046	+0.5
Computer Science	49,656	-3.4
Economics	40,596	+1.4
Electrical Engineering	49,926	-0.9
Information Systems	42,108	-3.7
Marketing	36,071	+1.9
Mechanical Engineering	49,088	+0.9

The Big Picture

Your college search should start with a first and second choice of majors in case you decide your initial choice is not a good fit. Once you are happy with your choice of majors, you can start looking for schools that offer the top ranked programs for those majors at a price and location you will be happy with.

If you are starting at the ground floor—meaning you do not have a specific field of study in mind—you need to understand the components that fuel a successful college education for all majors:

Make technology part of your education

Scientists, doctors, computer programmers and chemists are not the only people who need to understand technology. In every field—that includes the arts, journalism, and teaching—you need to embrace computers and the Internet. A variety of computer skill sets may put you ahead of other candidates in a tight job market, so factor some type of computer education into your college plan.

Prepare for a lifetime of career change

Perhaps you know a friend or relative who has lost a job, been laid off, or forced to retire at an early age. This was not common a generation ago, but it certainly is now. The truth is that today's college students have to be prepared not only for one career, but for several. That is not meant to confuse or depress you—many people make the decision to change careers because it makes them happier! But when you are selecting a major, make sure it is in an area that gives you the versatility to switch career paths if you choose to or are forced to later on in life.

Get the most for your money

Everyone knows that college is not cheap. In the introduction of this book, you saw how high the average tuition and fees were at public and private institutions. And that is what makes the right selection of a major so important on your way in—if you select the right major and then a college with a strong reputation in that field of study you will get the best education for your dollar.

Use your major to distinguish yourself

First, pick the right major for your skills and interests. Then pick a good school for that field of study. That does not mean picking the most expensive school or a school that is far from where you live. If you want to work in your home town, picking a home town school with a competitive program gives you access to instructors who work for local employers. This is a great way to build a network that will help you land a job while you are still in college or after graduation.

Read, read, and read

With the Internet, it is now possible to find a lot of information about specific majors at a college. It also helps you anticipate changes in your chosen field—whether you are picking a college major at age 18 or thinking about a career change at age 30 or 40. Get into the habit of reading newspaper and business stories about all sorts of career fields.

Be prepared to go back to school later in life

You might have heard this expression already—"lifetime learning." If you have not, get used to it. Experts predict that the average 18-year-old may have three to five completely different careers by the time she retires, so that means you may be going back to school at many points in your life. Make sure the major and school you choose gives you the best background for the training you might need later. Get the best education the first time around so retraining might mean a few new courses instead of an expensive, lengthy new degree! Be sure your choice of college is fully accredited in your field of study.

The Shocking Cost of Changing a Major

What would you say if a total stranger walked up to you and demanded $75,000? You would yell for the police, right? Believe it or not, that can be the cost of changing majors one or more times before graduation.

In reality $75,000 is sometimes the minimum. Consider this—a change in major might delay graduation a year or two. If you attend a public university, that cost tacks on an additional $8,000-$16,000 in tuition and fees alone. Add on housing and room and board costs of $10,000 to $20,000 and you can see the real expense. This is the cost before even considering the interest costs on another student loan.

So where is the rest of the $75,000? Lost income. Go back to the chart on page 10, and take a look at those starting salaries; that is the amount of money you would be failing to earn while spending another year in school. This is called an opportunity cost for opportunity missed.

Lost wages are not the only lost money—you also lose the chance to invest in benefits like 401[k] plans and other savings and investments that grow over time. That cuts into your ability to buy a house, provide for your family, and plan for retirement. While all those goals may be years away, you will be amazed at how fast time goes by! You will also be losing valuable on-the-job experience and the acquisition of on-the-job time required for promotions and to qualify for graduate school tuition assistance.

Despite all this potential loss, studies show that anywhere from 40-60 percent of college students will still change their majors two to three times before graduation. This book will help you avoid these costly decisions.

The Good News

Some people make selecting a college major sound more difficult than it really should be. After 12 years of school, you should have a pretty good understanding of what your strengths and interests are. If you have always been strong in math, it would make sense to first look at math and other quantitative fields for career options. If you are a talented writer and communicator, you'll find dozens of fields that require these abilities.

It is amazing how many students who have struggled with math or other quantitative subject areas in high school suddenly begin selecting college majors that are related to the subjects that gave them so much trouble. In college, once they realize that they still hate math, they are in crisis and have to switch to a new major or a new college entirely. This does not have to happen to you.

The key to finding the right major, like all things in life, is knowing yourself. You should dream big and think imaginatively about your future, but by all means, play to your strengths. Choose a major that will help you develop those strengths and take them into new and satisfying directions. You will be happier that way and probably much more successful in life.

Where to Start

You have already started—you are reading this book! But there are many other resources for you to explore that will help you find your major choices. There are great resources on the Internet alone—several sites are listed under each major in the back of the book. You can also ask your teachers and counselors to help you find professionals to talk to in fields related to the majors that interest you. Ask people working in these fields how much they like their work and how much training it took them to get the jobs they have. Find out where they see their careers going in the future. Most important, ask them what they *do not* like about what they are doing—that can teach you a great deal!

You are encouraged to take every assessment survey in this book. Some will ask what seem like similar questions, but there is a point to this—you need to compare your alternative choices on a number of scales. Actually, your school counselor or your local community college might have other tools you can use to help you determine your possible choices—just ask them. They are there to help you—take full advantage of that!

You can also take exploratory coursework at a community college to see if your major fits you. Many students today are taking college coursework while still in high school. They are getting a head start on their higher education.

Does my major fit me?

Right now, you might have a few ideas of possible majors and you will get the chance to test those choices in various ways throughout this book. For this first exercise select your current top major choice. Begin by asking yourself the following list of questions on about your top choice. Use your best guess for each item. There are no right answers. This is just a thought starter.

(Top Major Choice)

1. Do my past grades indicate I can do the work this major requires?

   _____

   _____

2. Will this major lead to a career that will meet my future lifestyle expectations?

   _____

   _____

3. What do I expect a college education in this field to do for me?

   _____

   _____

4. Can I handle the typical time commitment required to earn a marketable degree?

   _____

   _____

5. Are my study skills good enough to help me be successful at learning the coursework?

   _____

   _____

6. How does this major relate to what I have always wanted to be when I grew up?

   _____

   _____

Chapter Summary:

- Changing a major can cost $75,000, including lost income!
- Take a hard look at your high school grades to get a good idea of what subjects you will excel in when you get to college.
- Read as much as you can about the field you want to study and then take the time to talk to counselors, teachers, and workers who know that field.

Where to Surf:

- The College Board: www.collegeboard.com
- Sallie Mae: www.collegeanswer.com

CHAPTER 2

■■■■■■■■■■■■■■■■■■■

THE 10-CLUSTER SYSTEM:
LOOKING AT YOUR MAJOR
IN A WHOLE NEW WAY

If you have spent any time talking to your high school counselor about your future plans, you might have heard the term "career clusters." These are groups of careers built around specific skills or academic disciplines. They are a fairly useful way to start career planning.

The approach of this book, however, is a little different. By picking your *major* first instead of a career field, you will have a better strategy to pick the right college and later the right career. For example, an individual may have a career goal to become a high school principal, teacher, counselor, psychologist, or coach. All are different careers, yet they share a set of common college major choices. They would each be in different career clusters. In this book they are in similar major clusters.

It is not that thinking about a career is not important – it is just that dreaming about a career and deciding on the training you will need for that career are two dramatically different things. If you decide on a career without examining the coursework necessary to earn the degree in a preparatory field, you might find that the career is not so interesting after all.

Case in point: If you want to become a doctor because you really want to help people but do not really love science, you are bound to be disappointed. Why? Because, doctors deal with science every day. Wanting to help people is an important part of being a doctor, but it is really only part of what qualifies you for that career. Students who plan to enter medical school often major in biology or chemistry.

What the 10-Cluster System Does

The 10-Cluster System groups all of the majors into one of ten families, or clusters, based on shared characteristics. (You will find some majors appearing in more than one cluster, but they are rare cases.) Clusters are not built around job/career tracks. These clusters are based on the *academic ability, behavioral patterns, interests, and required coursework* you will need to succeed in a field of study at the college level. They also reflect expectations of the college experience.

The 10-Cluster System breaks down into four *quantitative* clusters (involving science, numbers and computation) and six *qualitative* clusters (made up of social studies, language, and the arts).

Why pick a cluster first? Because, as you fully analyze your major choices, you will see subject areas that are similar to one another. Several fields will meet a number of your criteria. Reviewing these related subjects will give you more options. Majors in the same cluster will have many characteristics in common and may be equally attractive to you.

In Chapters 5 and 9, you will see majors sorted among each of the ten following clusters:

Cluster #1: Applied Technology

Applied Technology majors focus on technical skills that can be directly applied to solving problems, enhancing results, building systems, and managing projects. Because these majors are so directly tied to actual job descriptions, the average time to earn a marketable degree varies greatly ranging from two years for an associate degree to four or five years for a bachelors degree. The demands of the job market actually dictate the level of education required.

Examples: Computer Science and Architectural Engineering

Cluster #2: Computational

The majors in this cluster usually require a bachelors degree or higher and are focused on management and information processing. They require strong computational, modeling, financial, and structured logic skills, but not (necessarily) the highest level of math coursework.

Examples: Accounting, Marketing, and Business Administration

Cluster #3: Science-Related

Majors in this group are heavily weighted toward professional or graduate foundation education. They cover the physical, natural, and biological sciences as well as related professional fields—primarily in healthcare areas.

Examples: Medicine, Dentistry, and Biology

Cluster #4: Allied Health

Allied health majors prepare individuals for health professions that assist doctors, dentists, pharmacists, and other healthcare professionals. These individuals are trained to work with patients in medical testing and laboratory procedures. Students need to take some science course work, but their training is focused on highly specialized job skills.

Examples: Physical Therapy, Medical Assisting, and Medical Records

Cluster #5: Social Sciences

Social science majors often need a graduate education to secure jobs directly related to their fields of study. They study subjects related to human behavior, statistics, social systems, cultures, and human development.

Examples: Psychology, Sociology, and Political Science

Cluster #6: Human Services

The largest major group in this cluster is education, but this category also contains a wide range of majors that provide direct assistance to people, often in the public sector.

Examples: Education, Law Enforcement, Human Resources, and Social Work

Cluster #7: Language

Languages, literature, and other forms of communication majors form this cluster. The time to earn a marketable degree for majors in this cluster often exceeds four years.

Examples: Modern Languages, Linguistics, and English Literature

Cluster #8: Verbal

Spoken communication skills are central to this cluster. These majors tend to focus on face-to-face skills – communicating with the public, gathering and interpreting information for written and visual media, and developing critical-thinking skills. Majors in this field tend to end up in professional schools or a graduate program in a specialized area.

Examples: Journalism, Law, Real Estate, and Publishing

Cluster #9: Fine/Professional Arts

Almost all the majors in this cluster require graduate education and high-level performance proficiency to achieve job-ready-level skills. These fields develop and foster very specialized artistic talents of individuals.

Examples: Theater, Fine Arts, and Dance

Cluster #10: Technical Arts

Most of these majors develop specific job skills that can be completed at the two-year, associate degree level. The majors are related to food service, art, and fashion.

Examples: Culinary Arts, Graphic Arts and Design, Interior Design, and Fashion Design

Assessing the Basic Components of a Specific Major

The 10-Cluster System was developed using the criteria that follows. It can be insightful to see how a major choice of yours stacks up based on these ten criteria. If you already have a major in mind, take some time to answer these questions about it. Three copies of this self-assessment worksheet are provided for you to use.

(Major to be Analyzed)

This self-assessment will help you begin to see how you feel about the criteria used to sort the various fields of study. Answer each question in terms of the major you selected for analysis. Answer to the best of your ability without seeking information from other sources.

1. Think about the people you know who have been successful studying in this field. What do they have in common?

   _____

   _____

   _____

   _____

2. What type of high school course work will qualify you for study in this field?

   _____

   _____

   _____

   _____

3. Where will the jobs be for graduates of this major and what will they pay?

_____

_____

_____

_____

4. Will this major support your career development over a decade or more, or will it lead to a profession that you will only have for a few years?

_____

_____

_____

_____

5. How difficult is the coursework in this field?

_____

_____

_____

_____

6. What types of specialized skills will you develop studying in this area?

_____

_____

_____

_____

7. What types of things do people majoring in this field read?

    _____

    _____

    _____

    _____

8. How likely are you to meet the admission requirements to study at a
    leading school in this field?

    _____

    _____

    _____

    _____

9. Will the skills you develop in this major be transferable to other fields?

    _____

    _____

    _____

    _____

10. What other courses will you need to take outside of your major to
    graduate?

    _____

    _____

    _____

    _____

(Major to be Analyzed)

This self-assessment will help you begin to see how you feel about the criteria used to sort the various fields of study. Answer each question in terms of the major you selected for analysis. Answer to the best of your ability without seeking information from other sources.

1. Think about the people you know who have been successful studying in this field. What do they have in common?

   _____

   _____

   _____

   _____

2. What type of high school course work will qualify you for study in this field?

   _____

   _____

   _____

3. Where will the jobs be for graduates of this major and what will they pay?

   _____

   _____

   _____

   _____

4. Will this major support your career development over a decade or more, or will it lead to a profession that you will only have for a few years?

_____

_____

_____

_____

5. How difficult is the coursework in this field?

_____

_____

_____

_____

6. What types of specialized skills will you develop studying in this area?

_____

_____

_____

_____

7. What types of things do people majoring in this field read?

_____

_____

_____

_____

8. How likely are you to meet the admission requirements to study at a leading school in this field?

_____

_____

_____

_____

9. Will the skills you develop in this major be transferable to other fields?

_____

_____

_____

_____

10. What other courses will you need to take outside of your major to graduate?

_____

_____

_____

_____

(Major to be Analyzed)

This self-assessment will help you begin to see how you feel about the criteria used to sort the various fields of study. Answer each question in terms of the major you selected for analysis. Answer to the best of your ability without seeking information from other sources.

1. Think about the people you know who have been successful studying in this field. What do they have in common?

    _____

    _____

    _____

    _____

2. What type of high school course work will qualify you for study in this field?

    _____

    _____

    _____

    _____

3. Where will the jobs be for graduates of this major and what will they pay?

    _____

    _____

    _____

    _____

4. Will this major support your career development over a decade or more, or will it lead to a profession that you will only have for a few years?

    _____

    _____

    _____

    _____

5. How difficult is the coursework in this field?

    _____

    _____

    _____

    _____

6. What types of specialized skills will you develop studying in this area?

    _____

    _____

    _____

    _____

7. What types of things do people majoring in this field read?

    _____

    _____

    _____

    _____

8. How likely are you to meet the admission requirements to study at a leading school in this field?

_____

_____

_____

_____

9. Will the skills you develop in this major be transferable to other fields?

_____

_____

_____

_____

10. What other courses will you need to take outside of your major to graduate?

_____

_____

_____

_____

If you have other major choices that hold some interest to you, go back and answer the same ten questions based on that new potential major choice.

Chapter Summary:

Finding a major cluster that is right for you is the first step in picking the right major, and eventually, the right school for you. Why? Once you find the subject area in which you are most interested, you can correctly select the school that meets your quality, location, and affordability test.

Where to Surf:

- MonsterCollege: college.monster.com
- The College Board: myroad.collegeboard.com/myroad/navigator.jsp
- Sallie Mae: www.collegeanswer.com

CHAPTER 3

■■■■■■■■■■■■■■■■■■■■

TIME TO GRADUATION

Time is money—and that is why planning your time to graduation is critically important. First of all, most of us do not have unlimited funds to spend on tuition or unlimited time that we want to dedicate to college. You need to develop an action plan that fits your unique situation. There are many different ways to earn your college degree. Some students prefer a two-year course of study that will qualify them for employment. For these students, it is often a way to start earning money as they continue to study on a part-time basis. Others look at combined bachelors/masters programs that may get them out of school in as little as a total of five years with a graduate degree without the extra expense of separate graduate study. These are just two examples of the many types of non-traditional approaches to higher education that exist today.

In Chapter 5, you will get your first look at the majors that fit into each cluster in The 10-Cluster System. You will also see that those groupings are broken down by time to earn a degree. Within each cluster are majors that can lead to degrees in approximately two, four, or six years of study. The time it will take to earn a degree related to a job. If finding a job related to what you studied is not an important consideration for you, you may earn your degree in a field at several different exit points.

Over 80 percent of today's college students are considered non-traditional. They are attending college in a pattern other than the traditional four years of daytime, full-time study.

As you narrow down your fields of interest, you must simultaneously look at timing issues. How long do you plan to be in college? Ask yourself:

- Can I afford the tuition required for the time it takes to graduate in this major?
- Do I actually want to stay in school as long as this major requires?
- Do I have an option to do some coursework in this field that will qualify me for entry-level employment and then return to school on a part-time basis while working to earn a higher level degree?

Even if you think you understand the types of degrees that schools offer and how much time they typically take to complete, it is worth going over the various alternative enrollment patterns to determine how they will benefit you.

Degrees in Less than Four Years

While it is possible to complete a baccalaureate degree in less than four years, it usually takes longer. Typically, those graduating in less than four years will be earning some other degree. These pre-baccalaureate programs come in two varieties:

1. *Certificate or Diploma programs* are non-degree programs. They provide specific, specialized training in a short period of time. People take certificate courses to learn a specialized career or life skill. For instance, people take a sequence of classes in computer software so they can become certified in certain software packages.

2. *Associate Degree majors* feature courses of study that may be similar to the first two years of study at a four-year college. Students often use the credits earned to transfer to a four-year institution that offers more advanced coursework. Community colleges and some four-year institutions offer associate degrees to students who want to develop a specialized skill in a short time. The main types of associate degrees are:
   • Associate of Arts [AA]
   • Associate of Science [AS]
   • Associate of Applied Science [AAS]

Four- to Six-Year Degrees

Bachelors degrees are typically earned after a four- to six-year course of study. They are called four-year degrees out of tradition. In the past, most students finished college degree requirements in four years. That is not the case for most of today's students. Baccalaureate degrees come in many varieties. The two most common are:
   • Bachelor of Arts [BA]
   • Bachelor of Science [BS]

Degrees in Six Years or More

Professional and graduate degree majors complete academic requirements to become licensed in a recognized profession, such as medicine or law or develop advanced credentials in a specialized field through research and empirical learning. Typically, these students have earned a college degree before beginning to work on their graduate coursework.

In selecting a college major, it is important to understand how long it will take you to earn a marketable degree. Are you ready to commit to two, four, or six years or more of college? In every cluster there are options. You can find programs in each grouping that should meet your desired time commitment. This is another reason to first focus on a cluster instead of single majors.

Chapter Summary:

Over 80 percent of today's college students are considered non-traditional. They are attending college in a pattern other than the usual four years of daytime, full-time study while enrolled.

For More Information:

Viollt, Michael P. *100 Ways to Cut the High Cost of Attending College (Money-Saving Advice for Students and Parents)*. Cooper Square Press. New York, NY. 2002

CHAPTER 4

■ ■ ■ ■ ■ ■ ■ ■ ■ ■ ■ ■ ■ ■ ■ ■ ■ ■ ■ ■

FIND YOUR MAJOR

Expectations Survey

What will your college education do for you?

Now that you have reviewed the importance of time to earn a degree, the next instrument will help you look at what you expect to get out of the time you will spend in college. Try to answer each item quickly and go with your first-choice response. There are no wrong or right answers.

If the item listed is an important outcome of your college education, circle the letter (either "A" or "B") under the **Important** heading. If it is not, circle the letter (either "A" or "B") under the **Not Important** heading. When you are undecided, go with the response that is closest to your expectation. You need to make a selection for all fourteen items.

Your College Education Should Help You Achieve:

	Not Important	Important
1. An understanding of different cultures	A	B
2. A starting salary that is above the average for college graduates	B	A
3. A set of life values and goals	A	B
4. Mastery of an applied skill	B	A
5. A complete set of career-related skills	B	A
6. Admission to a professional school (dentistry, medicine, law, etc.)	A	B

	Not Important	Important
7. A professional license or certification	B	A
8. An appreciation of the liberal arts	A	B
9. A strong background in the humanities and literature	A	B
10. A greater-than-average number of job opportunities at graduation	B	A
11. An understanding of your historical heritage	A	B
12. A job related to what you studied	B	A
13. Strong research skills	A	B
14. A clearly identified career path	B	A

Now, total the number of "A's" and "B's" that you have circled and put the results on the lines below. Be sure to count all the "A's" and "B's" because they are not always in the same column.

Total Number of A's _____

Total Number of B's _____

These results give you an indication of where you should begin your exploration of the right major for you. Individuals with more "A's" than "B's" tend to see college more as a time to build career and job opportunities. Those with more "B's" than "A's" may also be career-oriented but see college, first, as a place to grow as an individual. For this group, college must focus on the world around them—past, present, and future.

In either case, the next section will help you identify the cluster that best meets your interests and abilities.

- If your *A's scored higher* on the expectations survey that you just finished, complete the **CLUSTER SURVEY A** starting on the following page.
- If your *B's scored higher,* skip ahead to the **CLUSTER SURVEY B**.

Cluster Survey A

For each group of three statements that follows, select the one from the group that "best" describes you. Even if they all appear to be poor matches with your interests and abilities select the "best" of the group for you. Put a check mark in the box in front of the selected item.

1. ☐ You enjoy solving problems   ✪
    ☐ You have artistic ability   ■
    ☐ Reading helps you learn about people   ▣

2. ☐ You are good at expressing yourself   ☒
    ☐ Puzzles and quizzes can be fun   ◉
    ☐ You enjoy being the center of attention   ■

3. ☐ You are comfortable with routine   ●
    ☐ You find it easy to communicate with others   ☒
    ☐ Solving word problems is like a game   ◉

4. ☐ Exploring others' feelings and emotions is interesting   ▣
    ☐ You like to see what makes things work   ✪
    ☐ Business/financial information attracts your attention   ●

5. ☐ Most math concepts are easy to understand   ✪
    ☐ You have a special artistic talent   ■
    ☐ World news is of great interest to you   ▣

6. ☐ Science is your favorite subject   ◉
    ☐ Drama and theater interest you   ■
    ☐ You find it easy to persuade others   ☒

7. ☐ Speaking before a group can be fun   ☒
    ☐ You like to build things   ✪
    ☐ A neat working environment is critical   ●

8. ☐ You enjoy doing science research ⊙
    ☐ News about other countries draws your attention ▣
    ☐ You enjoy drawing ■

9. ☐ You often try to improve the way things are done ✪
    ☐ Working with large groups of people is fun ▣
    ☐ Experiments are interesting ⊙

10. ☐ Assembling items from instructions can be relaxing ✪
    ☐ You enjoy reading fiction ☒
    ☐ You enjoy trying new looks and styles ■

11. ☐ Learning about human health is interesting ⊙
    ☐ You like classroom discussions ☒
    ☐ You enjoy creating things for others ■

12. ☐ You like to establish a plan and follow it in detail ✪
    ☐ You prefer to work with guidelines ●
    ☐ Your writing skills are above average ☒

13. ☐ Learning about investments interests you ●
    ☐ You enjoy helping others ▣
    ☐ Art is a favorite pastime ■

14. ☐ You enjoy facts and statistics ●
    ☐ Technical reading bores you ☒
    ☐ You read science-related magazines for fun ⊙

15. ☐ You enjoy making a logical argument ●
    ☐ Helping someone with her school work can be fun ▣
    ☐ You have always been able to express yourself in writing ☒

16.   ☐ Outlining material is an easy task   ●
      ☐ You enjoy different art forms   ■
      ☐ Statistics related to sports interests you   ✪

17.   ☐ Working with numbers is more interesting than reading   ✪
      ☐ Others look to you for help with their diet and nutrition   ⊙
      ☐ Foreign languages come very easily to you   ⊠

18.   ☐ Learning about animals is interesting   ⊙
      ☐ You tend to do well in courses that require
          a lot of writing   ⊠
      ☐ You are highly organized   ●

19.   ☐ Mathematic problems can become a game   ✪
      ☐ Reading about people's attitudes and opinions
          is enjoyable   ▣
      ☐ Performing in front of others is fun   ■

20.   ☐ Solving science problems is interesting   ⊙
      ☐ Your strength seems to lie in English class   ⊠
      ☐ You keep a "to do" list of things to accomplish   ●

21.   ☐ Understanding why others do things is important   ▣
      ☐ You enjoy creating stories   ■
      ☐ You are interested in business   ●

22.   ☐ You enjoy working with children   ▣
      ☐ You can easily follow a set of written directions   ✪
      ☐ Banking and finance hold some interest for you   ●

23.   ☐ You search for new artistic experiences   ■
      ☐ You have a need to help other people   ▣
      ☐ The scientific process used by scientists fascinates you   ⊙

24. ☐ Your standardized test scores are highest in the
science section ◉

☐ Building designs interests you ✪

☐ Opportunities to meet people from different
backgrounds are exciting ▣

TOTALS: Add up the number of times you selected an item that was followed by a ✪ and write that total in the space provided below for that category. Then do the same thing for each of the other symbols.

✪	**Applied Technology**	____
●	**Computational**	____
◉	**Allied Health**	____
☒	**Verbal**	____
■	**Technical Arts**	____
▣	**Human Services**	____

The cluster with the highest total is your top cluster choice. Your interests and abilities best match those of people who have been successful in the fields of study represented by that cluster. If you have the same or nearly the same scores in two or more clusters, you may want to review both or all of them. You should now go on to Chapter 5 to begin to preview the majors that make up your top scoring cluster.

Cluster Survey B:

For each group of statements that follows, select the one that "best" describes you. Even if they all appear to be poor matches with your interests and abilities select the "best" of the group for you. Put a check mark in the box in front of the selected item.

1. ☐ Speaking before a group can be fun ◆
   ☐ You have artistic ability ▲
   ☐ Reading helps you learn about people ❖

2. ☐ You are good at expressing yourself ◆
   ☐ Puzzles are fun ✳
   ☐ You like being the center of attention ▲

3. ☐ Exploring others' feelings and emotions is interesting ❖
   ☐ You find it easy to communicate with others ◆
   ☐ You enjoy drawing ▲

4. ☐ Most math concepts are easy to understand ✳
   ☐ You have a special artistic talent ▲
   ☐ World news is of great interest to you ❖

5. ☐ Your favorite subject in school is science ✳
   ☐ Drama and theater interest you ▲
   ☐ You find it easy to persuade others ◆

6. ☐ Languages are easy to learn ◆
   ☐ Working with large groups of people is fun ❖
   ☐ Experiments are interesting ✳

7. ☐ News about other countries draws your attention ❖
   ☐ You enjoy reading fiction ◆
   ☐ Your choice is to have freedom while you work ▲

8.
- ☐ Solving math problems has always been easy ✳
- ☐ You like classroom discussions ◆
- ☐ You have a special interest in performing musically ▲

9.
- ☐ Science is your strength ✳
- ☐ You enjoy helping others ❖
- ☐ Art is a favorite pastime ▲

10.
- ☐ You read a lot ◆
- ☐ Learning about other cultures is interesting ❖
- ☐ Science is a favorite subject ✳

11.
- ☐ You read science-related magazines for fun ✳
- ☐ Your writing skills are above average ◆
- ☐ Analyzing people's behavior interests you ❖

12.
- ☐ You enjoy trying new looks and styles ▲
- ☐ Helping someone with his/her school work can be fun ❖
- ☐ Technical reading bores you ◆

13.
- ☐ You have always been able to express yourself in writing ◆
- ☐ You enjoy various art forms ▲
- ☐ Building science projects is an interesting assignment ✳

14.
- ☐ Performing in front of others is fun ▲
- ☐ Others look to you for help with math ✳
- ☐ Foreign languages come very easily to you ◆

15.
- ☐ Learning about animals is interesting ✳
- ☐ You tend to do well in courses that require a lot of writing ◆
- ☐ Reading about people's attitudes and opinions is enjoyable ❖

16. ☐ You enjoy creating stories   ▲

    ☐ Your strength seems to lie in English class   ◆

    ☐ Understanding why others do things is important   ❖

17. ☐ You enjoy working with children   ❖

    ☐ You search for the meaning in a conversation   ◆

    ☐ Solving word problems requires a system   ✳

18. ☐ You search for new artistic expressions   ▲

    ☐ You have a need to help other people   ❖

    ☐ The scientific process fascinates you   ✳

19. ☐ Your standardized test scores were highest in
      the math section   ✳

    ☐ You enjoy performing for a crowd   ▲

    ☐ Opportunities to meet people from different
      backgrounds are exciting   ❖

20. ☐ You learn valuable lessons about life from nature   ✳

    ☐ Learning about other cultures interests you   ❖

    ☐ You enjoy expressing your opinion in a group   ▲

TOTALS: Add up the number of times you selected an item that was followed by a ◆ and write that total in the space provided below for that category. Then do the same thing for each of the other symbols.

◆ **Language**   _____

❖ **Social Sciences**   _____

▲ **Fine/Professional Arts**   _____

✳ **Science-Related**   _____

The cluster with the highest number after it is your top cluster choice. Your interests and abilities best match those of people who have been successful in the fields of study represented by that cluster. If you have the same or nearly the same scores in two or more clusters, you may want to review both or all of them.

Chapter Summary:

- Your expectations for what a college education should deliver will impact your choice of field of study.

- It is necessary to take a close look at what you enjoy studying and doing when choosing a major cluster.

CHAPTER 5

■■■■■■■■■■■■■■■■■■

In this chapter, the individual majors that make up each of the ten clusters are presented. Each grouping of majors is made up of related fields of study. You should find that many majors in a cluster interest you. You will find information resources for each major in the last section of this book.

How to Use the Clusters

Record the scores from your cluster survey in the boxes provided below. Some items might have no score.

1.	Applied Technology	
2.	Computational	
3.	Science Related	
4.	Allied Health	
5.	Social Sciences	
6.	Human Services	
7.	Language	
8.	Verbal	
9.	Fine/Professional Arts	
10.	Technical Arts	

Take a closer look at the cluster that represents your highest score from the cluster survey. It is important to begin thinking in terms of clusters or groups. Many college students lack a clear understanding of how majors relate to one another and how related majors may be of interest to them.

For example, in the Computational cluster, the majors are highly structured, detail-oriented, based on logic and problem solving, and often require a great deal of work with numbers. Students who fit this profile will find a number of majors that are attractive within this cluster. Some other clusters contain majors that share traits with the computational cluster, but they have distinguishing qualities of their own as mentioned in earlier sections.

Within each cluster, different majors require various levels of study to earn a marketable degree. For some majors, the first marketable degree level is a certificate, for others, it's an associate or bachelors degree, and still others require graduate and post-graduate work. *Remember, a marketable degree means that average graduates at this level can find work in a field related to what they studied.* In other words, in some fields you only need an associate degree to get a job; others require a bachelors degree or higher.

An important consideration built into the linking of majors into clusters is how well a certain field prepares its graduates for both society's present and future needs. The majority of college freshmen indicate that the primary goal for their college education is the development of career opportunities that will serve them over a lifetime. According to Andrew Abbot in the University of Chicago magazine:

> "The one college experience variable that does have some connection with later worldly success is major. But most of that effect comes through the connection between major and occupation. The real variable driving worldly success, the one that shapes income more than anything else, is occupation."

It is estimated that 80 percent of the jobs requiring a college degree will be in fields or majors that will represent less than one-third of the college enrollments in 2010.

Start Using the 10-Cluster System

From the charts that follow, you will be able to pick out your highest scoring cluster and review the list of fields of study that it contains. Every college major offered at every school in the country is not listed on the chart. However, the majors presented represent the most popular choices you will see at most schools. They represent the major picks of 95 percent of all students and will be a good place to start comparing and contrasting the courses of study you might want to pursue.

Cluster #1: Applied Technology

Average Time to Earn a Degree Under 4 Years

- A/V Systems
- Computer-Aided Drafting
- Computer Applications
- Computer Maintenance
- Computer Networks
- Construction Technology
- Engineering Technology
- Environment Control Technology
- Heating and Air Conditioning Technology
- Mechanical Drafting
- Network Administration
- Network Management
- Security Systems
- Telecommunications
- Web Design

Average Time to Earn a Degree 4 to 6 Years ....

- Aerospace Engineering
- Agriculture
- Architectural Engineering
- Cartography/Surveying
- Chemical Engineering
- Civil Engineering
- Computer Programming
- Computer Science
- Computer Studies
- Electrical Engineering
- Electrical & Computer Engineering
- Environment Engineering
- Environmental Health Engineering
- Industrial Design
- Industrial Engineering
- Management Information Systems
- Material Science Engineering
- Math & Computer Science
- Mechanical Engineering
- Metallurgical Engineering
- Military Science
- Mining Engineering
- Naval Science
- Network Management
- Nuclear Engineering
- Petroleum Engineering
- Telecommunications Management
- Urban Planning

Average Time to Earn a Degree Over 6 Years ....

- Actuarial Science
- Architecture
- Meteorology

Cluster #2: Computational

Average Time to Earn a Degree Under 4 Years
- Computer Applications
- Computer Networks
- Environment Design
- Real Estate
- Records Management

Average Time to Earn a Degree 4 to 6 Years
- Accounting
- Business Administration
- Computer Programming
- Computer Systems
- Criminal Justice & Administration
- Database Management
- Database Programming
- Decision Support Systems
- Economics
- Finance
- Health Care Management
- Home Economics
- Hotel Management
- Institutional Administration
- International Business
- Management
- Marketing
- Statistics

Average Time to Earn a Degree Over 6 Years
- International Studies
- Law

Cluster #3:
Science-Related

Average Time to Earn a Degree Under 4 Years

No degree available in this time frame.

Average Time to Earn a Degree 4 to 6 Years.....................................
- Astronomy
- Biomedical Engineering
- Chemistry
- Forensic Science
- Forestry
- Oceanography
- Pharmacy Technology
- Physics
- Geology
- Zoology

Average Time to Earn a Degree Over 6 Years ....
- Anthropology
- Biochemistry
- Biology
- Botany
- Chiropractic
- Dentistry
- Earth Science
- Ecology
- General Science
- Health Science
- Medicine
- Microbiology
- Natural Science
- Optometry
- Pharmacy
- Physical Science
- Podiatry
- Veterinary Science

Cluster #4:
Allied Health

Average Time to Earn a Degree Under 4 Years

- Athletic Training
- Cardiovascular Technology
- Dental Assisting
- Dental Hygiene
- EEG Technology
- Fitness Specialist
- Health Assistant
- Massage Therapy
- Medical Administration
- Medical Assisting
- Medical Records
- Nuclear Medicine
- Practical Nurse (RN)
- Radiology Technology
- Respiratory Therapy
- Surgical Technology
- Veterinary Technology

Average Time to Earn a Degree 4 to 6 Years

- Kinetics
- Nursing
- Occupational Therapy
- Occupational Therapy Assisting
- Occupational Laboratory Technology
- Physical & Corrective Therapy
- Physical Education
- Physical Therapy
- Physical Training
- Recreational Therapy
- Sonography

Average Time to Earn a Degree Over 6 Years

No degree available in this time frame.

Cluster #5:
Social Sciences

Average Time to Earn a Degree Under 4 Years
No degree available in this time frame.

Average Time to Earn a Degree 4 to 6 Years.......................................
- Family Counseling
- General Studies
- Government
- Psychology
- Social Work

Average Time to Earn a Degree Over 6 Years ....
- African American Studies
- American Studies
- Asian Studies
- Counseling
- Geography
- History
- History & Philosophy of Science
- Jewish Studies
- Medieval Studies
- Philosophy
- Political Science
- Religion/Theology
- Sociology
- Theology
- Urban Studies
- Women Studies

Cluster #6:
Human Services

Average Time to Earn a Degree Under 4 Years

- Childcare Studies
- Dental Assisting
- Fitness Specialist
- Hospitality & Recreation
- Massage Therapy
- Medical Assisting
- Practical Nurse (RN)
- Social Work
- Travel

Average Time to Earn a Degree 4 to 6 Years..

- Coaching
- Criminology
- Drug Rehabilitation
- Education-Elementary
- Education-Music
- Education-Secondary
- Education-Teacher Aides/ Assistants
- Hospitality Management
- Human Resources
- Law Enforcement
- Organizational Studies
- Psychiatric Social Work
- Social Work
- Social Work Assistant

Average Time to Earn a Degree Over 6 Years ....

- Counseling
- Speech Therapy

Cluster #7: Language

Average Time to Earn a Degree Under 4 Years
No degree available in this time frame.

Average Time to Earn a Degree 4 to 6 Years..

- Linguistics
- Modern and Classical Language
- Modern Languages-Arabic
- Modern Languages-Chinese
- Creative Writing
- Modern Languages-French
- Modern Languages-German
- Modern Languages-Italian
- Modern Languages-Russian
- Modern Languages-Spanish

Average Time to Earn a Degree Over 6 Years.....................................

- Arts & Letters-General
- Classical Languages-Greek
- Classical Languages-Latin
- English Literature
- Modern and Classical Languages

Cluster #8:
Verbal

Average Time to Earn a Degree Under 4 Years
- Administrative Assistant
- Court Reporting
- Health Information Technology
- Law - Paralegal Studies
- Real Estate
- Records Management

Average Time to Earn a Degree 4 to 6 Years..
- Journalism
- Library Science
- Publishing
- Speech Language Pathologist
- Web Design
- Technical Writing

Average Time to Earn a Degree Over 6 Years ....
- Law

Cluster #9:
Fine/Professional Arts

Average Time to Earn a Degree Under 4 Years
No degree available in this time frame.

Average Time to Earn a Degree 4 to 6 Years......................................
- Art and Design
- Creative Writing
- Digital Media Technology
- Film/TV
- Sculpting

Average Time to Earn a Degree Over 6 Years ....
- Art
- Art History
- Art Pre-Professional
- Dance
- Film Study
- Fine Arts
- Music Composition
- Music-Instrumental
- Music-Vocal
- Speech & Drama
- Theater

Cluster #10:
Technical Arts

Average Time to Earn a Degree Under 4 Years
- Animation
- Broadcasting
- Cosmetology
- Culinary Arts
- Horticulture Science
- Interior Design
- Landscaping
- Media Arts
- Web Design

Average Time to Earn a Degree 4 to 6 Years..............................
- Fashion Design
- Fashion Merchandising
- Graphic Arts & Design
- Music Education
- Sports/Entertainment

Average Time to Earn a Degree Over 6 Years ....
No degree available in this time frame.

Major Selection Worksheets

What follows are three copies of a worksheet you can use to further focus your major choices. Now that you have completed the instruments in the earlier sections, you should be getting closer to narrowing down your top three major choices. For each of your top choices take some time to fill out the following worksheets. At this point, you may want to do some research to get information on each of your potential major choices.

Major Selection Worksheet

Name of Major:_____

1. Why are you interested in this major?

_____

_____

_____

2. Potential career fields commonly entered through this major:

_____

_____

_____

_____

3. Current job market for these career fields:

☐ Better than Average　　　☐ Average　　　☐ Below Average

4. Long-term income potential in these career fields:

☐ Exceeds your Expectations　☐ Meets your Expectations

☐ Below your Expectations

5. Type of college offering this major

_____

_____

6. How well do your abilities match with the required coursework in this major?

☐ Perfect Match　　☐ Okay Match　　☐ Poor Match

7. How well do your current interests match with the coursework in this major?

☐ Perfect Match　　☐ Okay Match　　☐ Poor Match

Major Selection Worksheet

Name of Major:_____

1. Why are you interested in this major?

_____

_____

_____

2. Potential career fields commonly entered through this major:

_____

_____

_____

_____

3. Current job market for these career fields:
   ☐ Better than Average   ☐ Average   ☐ Below Average

4. Long-term income potential in these career fields:
   ☐ Exceeds your Expectations   ☐ Meets your Expectations
   ☐ Below your Expectations

5. Type of college offering this major

_____

_____

_____

6. How well do your abilities match with the required coursework in this major?

   ☐ Perfect Match   ☐ Okay Match   ☐ Poor Match

7. How well do your current interests match with the coursework in this major?
   ☐ Perfect Match   ☐ Okay Match   ☐ Poor Match

Major Selection Worksheet

Name of Major:_____

1. Why are you interested in this major?

_____

_____

_____

2. Potential career fields commonly entered through this major:

_____

_____

_____

_____

3. Current job market for these career fields:

☐ Better than Average   ☐ Average   ☐ Below Average

4. Long-term income potential in these career fields:

☐ Exceeds your Expectations   ☐ Meets your Expectations
☐ Below your Expectations

5. Type of college offering this major

_____

_____

_____

6. How well do your abilities match with the required coursework in this major?

☐ Perfect Match   ☐ Okay Match   ☐ Poor Match

7. How well do your current interests match with the coursework in this major?

☐ Perfect Match   ☐ Okay Match   ☐ Poor Match

Chapter Summary:

- Your top scoring clusters should contain a number of majors of interest to you.

- An important consideration built into the linking of majors into clusters is how well a particular field prepares its graduates for society's present and future needs. It is estimated that 80 percent of the jobs requiring a college degree will be in fields or majors that will represent less than one-third of the college enrollments in 2010.

- With some additional research, you will begin to see how your top choices relate to the world of work and careers.

Where to Surf:

- Salary.com: For random information on various career salaries. www.Salary.com

SECTION 2

....

What Your Choice Means

CHAPTER 6

■■■■■■■■■■■■■■■■■■

FINDING THE SCHOOL THAT IS
RIGHT FOR YOU

If you have selected a cluster and have two to three majors within it on your list of potential fields of study, it is time to start thinking about the right schools for you.

Now that you know what you are shopping for, you can begin the process of searching for the best college fit. Use the following evaluation criteria to help select the best college or university for you:

- College reputation in your major field of study
- Overall reputation of the college a presented in standard reference publications
- Location and setting that you find pleasing
- Affordability
- College calendar that will get you to graduation
- Chance of being admitted based upon the strength of your application and supporting materials

One reason the best colleges and universities in the country earn their high ranking in a discipline is because they provide the best preparation for students in that field. Not everyone gets to go to Harvard or Yale, but guess what? Harvard and Yale do not necessarily provide the best or most marketable education in every field. It is possible that you will find the best education for you right in your own community.

To start the selection process, you need to decide on the type of college or university that is right for you.

The Three College "Brands"

No, this is not about McDonalds vs. Burger King, but as active consumers, you probably already know what defines a 'brand'—the sum total of all the important things that make a product or service unique. It is the look of something, the feel of it, and most important, its reputation. It is what makes Nike, well Nike. Knowing a brand means you already understand what you are buying.

If it were as easy to pick a college as it is to buy a pair of cross-trainers, you would not need to read this book. Believe it or not, colleges actually have their own brand identity. It is all about the school's philosophy of education and in the end, the quality of graduates it turns out. Before understanding an individual college brand, you need to understand the sector brands.

Colleges fall into three broad sector categories, or brand classes:

Career-Focused Colleges

Career-focused colleges emphasize class work directly applied to the world of work—students are career-ready when they graduate. At the same time, the good colleges in this group will also offer a strong component of general education or liberal arts course work. These institutions will have a large number of practitioner faculty who continue to work in their specialties while they teach. These programs are designed to provide the experiential learning and internship opportunities that make their graduates job-ready at the time of their graduation.

If you are thinking about a major in the Applied Technology, Allied Health, Technical Arts, and Computational clusters, you will likely be looking at career-focused colleges. These types of colleges, both public and private, are often found in mid to large cities. Cities offer an abundance of practitioner faculty and plenty of sites for internship experiences. These institutions range from institutes of technology and specialized schools of business to community colleges.

Foundation-Study Colleges

Foundation-Study colleges emphasize a preparatory, balanced curriculum for students who expect to enter career-focused education in graduate school. Students looking to continue their education in law, medicine, or dentistry typically enroll in these types of schools. Individuals who major in fields that require a masters or higher degree to enter the job market also would do well in these types of schools.

If your major choice is in the Science-Related, Social Sciences, or Language clusters, you should look at Foundation-Study schools. Liberal arts colleges and large research universities make up the largest grouping of these types of colleges.

Personal-Development Colleges

Personal-Development colleges are designed for students who want to develop special talents in writing, music, art or drama. These types of colleges mix liberal arts education with course work in the arts.

If your major choice is in the Fine/Professional Arts cluster you should look at Personal-Development schools, although students in majoring in this area often enroll in Foundation-Study colleges as well. Personal Development programs are typically found in smaller liberal arts colleges or within specialized schools at large universities.

Planning Early is Important

A *U.S. News and World Report* study points out that the average acceptance rate at colleges and universities nationwide is around 70 percent, but more freshmen than ever—nearly 1 in 10—now attend colleges that were their third or lower choice.

Why are students having to settle for choices that so far down their list? Because the number of applicants is rising, making admission more competitive. In fact, experts predict applications will rise faster than openings at most colleges through about 2010. There are several reasons for this trend:

- Birth rates surged during the 1980s and these children of baby boomers are now college age.

- A greater percentage of students (in every age group) are now going to college.

- An increasing number of older, first-time, and returning students are going to college to polish up their skills during a tough economy.

What Types of Students Do Colleges Want?

It makes sense for you to know what schools are looking for among all these applicants. According to the *Chronicle of Higher Education*, a publication for college administrators, admission officers review applications in different ways, depending on how selective their college is. Open admission schools require only a high school diploma and accept students on a first-come, first-served basis. Many community colleges have this policy. At the other extreme are very selective colleges like Harvard, Yale, and Princeton. They admit only a small percentage of applicants each year, sometimes fewer than 1 in 15 from a pool of very strong applicants. Most colleges fall somewhere in between these two extremes.

- *Less selective* schools generally have open enrollment policies that admit students as long as they meet certain minimum grade requirements. They generally use SAT® or ACT© scores for course placement only.

- *More selective* schools consider course work, grades, test scores, recommendations and essays for admission. They want to see whether you are ready for and enthusiastic about college-level study. These schools reject students who do not meet their admission criteria.

- *Very selective* schools have as many as 10 to 15 students applying for every spot in the entering class; their admission officers scrutinize every aspect of a student's high school experience, from academic strength to test scores. Since many applicants are strong academically, other factors—such as entrance essays are critical.

In no particular order, top colleges will want to see:

- What courses you took in high school
- Your grades and grade point average
- Your recommendations from counselors and teachers
- Your ethnicity
- Your answers to application questions
- Your response to at least one application essay
- Where you live (sometimes schools like to draw students from other areas of the country)
- How well you do in a personal interview
- If you have other family members who are alumni
- Your high school rank
- Your work experience
- Your extracurricular activities
- Your desired major
- Your admission test results
- Any special talents and skills you bring
- If you have participated in any volunteer activities

This type of scrutiny is why starting to think early about the right major and the right college for that major is so important. It is not unreasonable for high school students to start the application process in their sophomore and junior years. Starting to plan early will give you time to build a portfolio, gain volunteer experience, participate in activities, and establish reference relationships with teachers and counselors.

High school students do not need to become obsessed with the application process—some students fear that failing to get into their number one choice school means their lives will be ruined. Nothing could be more wrong. Most employers will tell you college is important, but the quality of the employee and her overall skills are far more important. Students should, however, give themselves the time they deserve to consider all their options—they should select the right majors first, and then select the right schools for those majors.

If You Have Selected Your Major, Start Building Your Application Timetable

The school selection process will not be examined in great detail—that is material for another book. Assuming, however, that you have arrived at your best alternatives for college majors, the following timetable may help you with the admission process.

During Y5our Junior Year:
- Make a list of potential college choices
- Visit colleges that interest you
- Sign up for the national exams that you plan or need to take—ACT, SAT, etc.
- Build a file system of college information
- In each file place a calendar of critical dates and deadlines

Fall of Your Senior Year:
- Begin to narrow your college choices down into categories—top choice, safety choice, middle choice, etc.
- Fill out your applications
- Discuss the college application process with teachers and counselors
- Take your standardized tests and make sure your scores are sent to each of your college choices
- If you are applying for Early Decision or Early Action programs, send in applications to these colleges
- Send in all applications
- Sign up to retake tests
- Make sure that transcripts, test scores, and reference letters have been sent to all the colleges you chose

Winter of Your Senior Year
- Keep working successfully at senior courses
- You should hear decisions on your Early Decision applications
- Have your school send mid-term grades to your college choices

Spring of Your Senior Year
- Send in your financial aid application
- Apply for student housing, if applicable
- Plan out how you intend to finance your college education
- Select your top college choice from those colleges that accepted you
- Attend orientation at your college
- Send your final grade report and/or official transcript to your college choice

Sticking to a Graduation Schedule

At the start of this book, it was pointed out that most students are taking, on average, more than five years to graduate from college. Some of the reasons for this are economic—many students need to work to put themselves through school and cannot attend college full time. Some students also take longer to graduate because recessionary budget cuts—particularly at public universities—have reduced the number of course sections being taught, which can make it difficult for students to enroll in required courses when they need to take them. These are justifiable reasons for taking longer to graduate.

You would think that colleges would welcome students spending all those extra tuition dollars, but administrators (especially those who work at public colleges and universities) are growing concerned about this trend. They realize that schools need to improve efficiency so they can free up classroom space for rising numbers of new students. In fact, the increasing size of high school graduating classes and the larger percentage of graduates going on to college are putting a real stress on higher education systems in many parts of the United States.

Some states are responding to these trends by creating incentives for on-time graduation, for example:

- In Texas, a new program approved by lawmakers will pay off the college loans of some students who graduate within the four-year limit. The program, dubbed "Texas-B-on-Time," requires students to demonstrate financial need and take a college-preparatory curriculum in high school. In return, the state provides them with zero-interest loans to cover the average annual cost of tuition, fees, books, and room and board. To keep their loans, students must maintain a 2.5 grade-point average in college and complete at least 75 percent of their credit hours attempted each semester.

- The University of Florida started a program in 1996 that guarantees a slot in any course required for a student's major. Students can track their academic records online and see how long it would take them to graduate if they change majors.

When selecting the colleges that offer your best choices of majors, check to see what incentives they offer for on-time graduation. Not only will you start your career sooner, but you will end up saving money in the long run. Each year, additional states will see the need to build special programs to encourage timely completion of college.

Chapter Summary:

- There are three basic types of colleges—Career-Focused, Foundation Study, and Personal Development.
- Take time to understand the types of admission qualifications your chosen college expects from you.
- Aiming for on-time graduation is crucial since every extra term costs dearly in extra tuition and lost wages. In addition, many colleges may start penalizing students who graduate late.

Where to Surf:

- U.S. News and World Report/Best College Rankings
  colleges.usnews.rankingsandreviews.com/best-colleges

CHAPTER 7

■■■■■■■■■■■■■■■■■

TAKING A REALISTIC LOOK
AT YOUR ABILITIES

Do you come from a family where everyone seems to follow in a similar career path? Do your parents, aunts, uncles, and cousins all seem to be engineers, doctors, teachers, or plumbers? There is nothing wrong with following in the family's footsteps if that is truly what you want to do. It is not unusual for family members to share traits and abilities that point them toward a particular field. That is what DNA is all about!

Ultimately, what you want to do with your life is about the unique you. You need to realistically assess your abilities and desires before picking a major. For instance, if you have a desire to be a doctor, you need to have a solid background in math and science. If you want to be a writer, you should have performed well—and enjoyed—your work in high school English literature and composition classes. Getting in touch with your abilities is a critical step in this process.

Past Performance = Future Returns

In this chapter, you will review what you have done in the past. This includes your grades, your high school rank and your test scores. These are indicators of how well you will do in school, as well as great tools to help you select your field of study. Looking back at classes and activities which you have enjoyed and done well in is the best way to get an idea of what things you will excel at in the future. Nothing predicts future events like past performance.

The Ability Matrix chart at the end of this chapter will give you some ideas about what types of academic performance and personal skills fit best in each clusters. Use this as a guidepost.

Here are some other indicators you can use:

Report Cards

Not everyone earns straight A's, but a look back through your academic records can provide a very good picture of where you have excelled academically and what areas you are likely to do well in the future. If you do not remember your past grades, you should pick up a copy of your transcript from your high school for this exercise.

Start by looking at all the classes in which you have earned B's or better. Generally, our best grades are in subjects we either find easy or like the most. The key here is not to focus on just the easy A's, but also the A's you worked for.

If you worked hard to earn a good grade in a subject, ask yourself—why did you do that? Was it because you liked the challenge of getting a good grade? Or was there something more? Did the class capture your interest for the whole term; maybe in a way you did not expect? Did you find yourself taking the next class in that subject? If so, how well did you do?

The point is not to just make a list of classes in which you did well—your grades tell you that—but to see *why* you excelled or performed poorly in certain classes and *why* you made certain choices afterward. Maybe you are the doctor's son who found himself in love with journalism or art. Or maybe you are the mechanic's daughter who found herself in love with computer science. Whatever you enjoy learning about is a strong indicator of what you should be considering as majors or minors in college.

High School Rank

Top colleges typically have their pick of the top 10 percent (by class rank) of high school graduates throughout the country. You have to understand, however, that your high class rank does not automatically qualify you for the top colleges and universities. First of all, it is a fact of life that students who attend top-ranked high schools (i.e., schools with richer academic resources and student bodies with higher test scores) tend to be viewed as more qualified applicants than students who come from high schools that are academically, economically, or resource deprived.

That means the quality of your high school can either work for you or against you. If you are valedictorian at a poor performing high school, your SAT and ACT results have to be good enough to put you in competition with students at better-quality schools. You will also need attention-getting extracurricular activities. Even then, you will probably have to work harder to make yourself attractive to the top colleges. This may not be fair, but it is the way it is.

That is where your teachers and counselors come in. If you have gone through the steps in Chapters 1-5 and narrowed down your choices of schools and majors, then make these people your allies and talk to them about your choices and alternatives.

- *Make sure your counselors and principals know who you are.* In most high schools, top students stand out, but if your school's enrollment is huge, don't be surprised if the administration or counselors do not know who you are. It is your job to make sure they get to know you—that is a lesson you will have to learn in the career world as well, so get used to it. Take the initiative and meet with counselors, advisors, department heads, teachers, and your principal. Tell them you want whatever assistance they can provide so that you can get into the right college program. The best educators are flattered when students ask for this kind of help, and they will bend over backwards to help you.

- *Make sure you start early.* It is not unreasonable to start lining up your support team in your sophomore or junior year of high school. Even if you are not applying to college until the fall of your senior year, these teachers, counselors and principals can keep you on point. If you are having trouble in certain classes, they are the people to talk to about getting help or refocusing your educational goals. Also, they can tell you about advanced placement courses and high school extracurricular programs that might improve your high school record and make you a stronger college applicant.

- *Make sure you make good allies outside of school.* Recommendations are an important part of most college applications. Employers, clergy, and professionals in the field you want to pursue are often good resources for college recommendations. So get to know good people in those roles and keep them apprised of your career goals, high school performance, and college plans.

ACT and SAT Scores

As much as everyone will tell you to calm down about these college admission tests, there is no denying how important they are in getting the attention of colleges. Why? A combined score of 25 or more on the ACT and 1200 or more on the SAT are minimum standards at top-ranked institutions. These scores are great equalizers that illustrate the quality of your high school. Students attend a wide variety of high schools but these tests are the same for everyone.

AP Credits

Advanced placement credits can help you place out of core undergraduate classes and allow you to graduate from college earlier. They also are a great way to experiment with potential college majors while still in high school. Many colleges look for good scores in this course work as an indicator that the applicant is motivated and will work harder than is required. If no one has approached you about advanced placement courses or if they are not offered in your high school, ask your guidance counselor how you might qualify to participate in these types of programs. You might also consider taking a course at your local community college while still enrolled in high school.

The Ability Matrix

Just as each college looks for specific combinations of abilities in the admission process, each major requires different combinations of abilities.

The following charts give you an idea of how your abilities and skills fit under The 10-Cluster System. Your general perception of your performance on these criteria is all the information you need to make use of this table.

Ability Matrix

What Ability Level is Needed for Each Major in Cluster #1-4 ?

Key:

■ *You should be in the top 25% of your HS class to major in this cluster.*

◆ *You need to be at least average on this trait.*

● *Not an important criteria for this cluster.*

	Cluster #1 Applied Technology	Cluster #2 Compu- tational	Cluster #3 Science- Related	Cluster #4 Allied Health
Academic Skills				
Math	■	◆	■	●
Science	■	◆	■	◆
Reading	◆	◆	◆	◆
Writing	◆	◆	◆	◆
Social Studies	●	●	●	●
Social Skills				
Communications/Speech	●	◆	◆	◆
Leadership	◆	◆	◆	◆
Team Building	●	●	●	◆
Listening Ability	◆	◆	◆	■
Special Talents				
Music, Art, Dance	●	●	●	●
Test Scores (ACT, SAT)				
Math	■	◆	■	●
Verbal	●	◆	◆	●

Ability Matrix

What Ability Level is Needed for Each Major in Cluster #5-7 ?

Key:

■ *You should be in the top 25% of your HS class to major in this cluster.*

◆ *You need to be at least average on this trait.*

● *Not an important criteria for this cluster.*

	Cluster #5 Social Sciences	Cluster #6 Human Services	Cluster #7 Language
Academic Skills			
Math	◆	●	●
Science	◆	●	●
Reading	◆	◆	◆
Writing	◆	◆	■
Social Studies	◆	◆	◆
Social Skills			
Communications/Speech	◆	◆	◆
Leadership	◆	◆	◆
Team Building	◆	■	●
Listening Ability	◆	■	■
Special Talents			
Music, Art, Dance	●	●	◆
Test Scores (ACT, SAT)			
Math	●	●	●
Verbal	◆	◆	◆

Ability Matrix

What Ability Level is Needed for Each Major in Cluster #8-10 ?

Key:

■ *You should be in the top 25% of your HS class to major in this cluster.*

◆ *You need to be at least average on this trait.*

● *Not an important criteria for this cluster.*

	Cluster #8 Verbal	Cluster #9 Fine/ Professional Arts	Cluster #10 Technical Arts
Academic Skills			
Math	●	●	●
Science	●	●	●
Reading	◆	◆	◆
Writing	■	●	●
Social Studies	●	●	●
Social Skills			
Communications/Speech	■	■	◆
Leadership	◆	◆	◆
Team Building	●	◆	■
Listening Ability	■	■	◆
Special Talents			
Music, Art, Dance	●	■	◆
Test Scores (ACT, SAT)			
Math	●	●	●
Verbal	◆	●	●

Chapter Summary

- You already have the tools to see where your interests and abilities lie—your report cards and test scores.

- Make an effort to build alliances with your guidance counselors, teachers, and administrators so when the time comes for you to apply for college they will have up-to-date information and you will have good recommendation options.

Where to Surf:

- About the SATs: www.collegeboard.com
- About the ACT: www.actstudent.org

CHAPTER 8

■■■■■■■■■■■■■■■■■■■

WHAT MAKES A DEGREE
MARKETABLE?

In Chapter 3, all of the majors in The 10-Cluster System were separated based on the time it takes to complete a marketable degree.

Degree programs and their curriculum are always changing. There is now more emphasis on programs with shorter completion times to graduation for mid-career students who are returning to college to upgrade their skills. There is also a move away from liberal arts graduate degrees to more career-focused advanced degrees. If you want proof, look no further than the proliferation of master's of business administration (MBA) programs over the past ten years.

Change, Change, and More Change

As you plan your future, the first question you need to answer is which world of work are you preparing for? Are you focusing on your place in the world of 2005 or the world of 2035? Most people agree that the world is changing exponentially faster, and will be a very different place in thirty years. For some of you reading this book, 2035 may only be the mid-point of your career!

You will need to be prepared for a world of work in which there will be one constant—change. It will be a world full of organizations that are continually reinventing themselves.

People will go in and out of jobs and careers. You will have a number of careers and a longer life, which will mean a chance to give more of your time as a volunteer after retirement in yet another career. Guess what—you will need training for that career, too.

Diversify Your Major

When selecting a major field of study, it is impossible to know what careers will be in demand in 2035. It is a pretty good bet that a core set of information processing skills will be an important ingredient in most career fields. These skills breakdown as follows:

- *Information Mining*—searching, categorizing, analyzing, and reporting of information
- *Information Relationship-Building*—how information is linked and what these links mean
- *Application of Information to Current Issues*—how information relates to real-world situations
- *Application of Information to Problem-Solving*—finding ways to use information to solve problems
- *Creation or Discovery of New Insights*—developing new insights by combining information sources to solve new, real-world issues and concerns
- *Ability to Articulate to Others*—the ability to express what has been discovered

The most sought after employee in the future will have the unique combination of (1) the strong information processing skills listed above and (2) highly specialized abilities in a specific career field.

This is why it is critical that you develop foundation skills along with your specialized education. All career fields are already experiencing changes brought on by this duality.

For instance, look at how these career areas have evolved:

- *Accounting* is no longer a control and audit function, but is now an analysis and decision-making process.
- *Teachers* are no longer needed as information experts in a particular subject area, but rather as facilitators for students' self-discovery.
- *Engineers* do not just apply formulas; they develop new approaches to problem-solving.
- *Doctors* do not just treat patients but collect, summarize, and interpret data.

Keep these changing skill sets in mind as you research the majors and minors in this book and review your alternatives.

Colleges have been slow to adjust their curriculum to this new merging of information processing with specialized training. If you do not find a college that offers this updated program design, consider designing your own program—by carefully planning a minor area of study that contributes to your development of information processing skill sets.

What Do Employers Want?

What a difference a few years can make. Turn back the clock to December 1999—the last few months of the technology bubble, the twilight of an unprecedented seven-year period of corporate and hiring growth. Students with specialized degrees—particularly computer science and masters in business administration (MBAs)—had their pick of great jobs, often two or three great jobs. In the struggle to fill positions in a fast-growing economy, few employers were insisting on superior communication and analytical skills along with job experience. They often were willing to settle for one or the other. Then the bottom fell out.

Since the recession began in 2000 and accelerated after 9/11, students have had to learn in a hurry what college graduates experienced back in the late 1970s and early 1980s—career-specific training is important, but a versatile education background, with strong job experience, will put you ahead of the pack.

Jeff Taylor, founder of the employment website Monster.com, puts it this way:

> *"Liberal arts training isn't enough, and neither is technical training. But you need both. The people who are getting jobs today are multi-dimensional. Say you're in marketing. That means you have these so-called 'soft skills' where you can easily communicate with people. But today, that's not enough. Your customers need you to understand databases...you need to have Web-based knowledge. If you are a tech major, you have to be good in a meeting and be able to express what you are doing in simple language. You need to be as good at communicating as you are at coding."*

What do employers want today? Two words: flexibility and ingenuity.

The Importance of the Liberal Arts

David A. Herron, chief executive officer of the Chicago Stock Exchange, is something of a rarity as a business leader. He never finished his under-graduate degree. That doesn't mean the one-time student at the University of California at Berkeley does not believe in the value of a college education. Herron explains:

> *"Just the other day, we were interviewing a guy who had impeccable credentials. He had a high-ranking MBA, an internship with a trading firm in Paris, qualifications that would have had him scooped up at any firm a few years ago. But the job market has changed, and we needed someone with broader experience. We're*

a Midwestern exchange, and he was too specialized in interna-
tional. The one thing I can say about college preparation and job
experience is not to over-specialize. And that's something people
should remember in good economic times and bad."

Herron admits "a weakness" for liberal arts graduates:

"The truth is that [stock] traders come from all sorts of educa-
tional backgrounds. That's why [he] was able to succeed without a
degree—you see quite a number of people in their 40s and 50s who
were able to make a career in this field without a degree. But even
that is changing. In any field today, you have to have the ability to
think, to analyze, to understand technology, and to see things that
may be outside your scope of current expertise. If I have one
criticism of new graduates, I find that so many students are trained
very well in a specific discipline, but they don't always have the
skills to think and work outside that discipline."

Most colleges—even in their associate degree programs—insist on some
basic liberal arts training. Taking a literature or creative writing course
should not be viewed as a necessary evil between your career-focused
classes. Courses that help you think, read, write, create, and speak should
be considered critical components of your career training.

Studies show a lack of such basic-skills education can cost you a chance
at a good job or, more important, a promotion later on.

Phil Pfeiffer, a computer and information sciences professor at East
Tennessee State University, conducted a 1998 survey of software, consult-
ing, and training firms to find out what they expected from applicants with a
BS or MS in computer science. His findings: Employers wanted "real"
experience—2 to 5 years of employment in the computer industry—but
they also wanted strong communication skills. What did his survey respon-
dents identify as strong communications skills?

- Strong written and spoken English
- The ability to help customers understand their requirements
- The ability to ask questions [not only in interviews, but in customer settings]
- The ability to respond to questions quickly, concisely, and simply
- The ability to "sell oneself"
- The ability to create clear metaphors that communicate a system's purpose

New graduates often lack these traits. You might say to yourself, well, that is just a problem for computer graduates. Wrong.

Paul O'Connor, executive director of World Business Chicago, a not-for-profit economic development corporation that counts CEOs from some of the city's largest companies as members, adds this viewpoint.

> *"Technology changes so fast. Everybody has to re-learn technology as it develops anyway. What employers want are graduates who have a broad base of skills that help them learn and change as their companies and industries change. You can repair a client's computers, but do you know how to work with clients face-to-face? Do you know how to listen to them and talk to them? Do you know how to anticipate their problems? That is the preparation that a broad-based education should give you."*

Where Jobs are Going

If you watch the news, you probably know that approximately 2.7 million U.S. manufacturing jobs were eliminated between 2000 and 2003, many of them going overseas. You have also probably heard that a growing number of white-collar jobs (e.g., phone-based customer service and software design) are moving to places like India, Singapore and Hong Kong, where English is spoken and the workforce is relatively well-educated.

Fortunately, not every U.S. job can be moved overseas. But the movement of these jobs proves one thing—companies can be a lot choosier about who they hire. They will pay top dollar for workers who know leading-edge technology in their field—and understand that every industry is built on information systems. But they will also demand that new hires demonstrate people skills, along with the ability to analyze and solve problems.

In fact, everyone will need these skills; not just the people headed for the corner office, but also secretaries, warehouse staffers—even waste haulers. Yes, someday, even trash collectors will probably need computer skills to do their jobs. As World Business Chicago's Paul O'Connor observes:

> *"Not everybody wants to be a CEO, but if you want at least a middle-class lifestyle in the next 10-20 years, you are going to have to commit to some college training and have an aptitude for analyzing situations and helping customers. For many workers, the associate degree is where the future is.*
>
> *The way certain jobs are moving overseas tells us a U.S. company's workforce is going to be its only sustainable advantage. Companies here are going to need workers at all levels who can*

*think on their feet and take the initiative with regard to training
and re-training. People will need cutting-edge skills in technology
specific to their job level and the ability to work face-to-face with
their customers. That's going to be the case whether you're a
secretary or a CEO."*

That is why O'Connor and other business experts believe that an associate degree—at a minimum—will be the ticket to what they call "the recreation of the nation's middle class." O'Connor says,

*"What young people need to realize is that the number of jobs that
used to go to people with only high school diplomas or a little bit
of college are fast disappearing. We're not only talking about
manufacturing or manual-labor jobs. We're talking about basic
white-collar jobs in this country that used to go to people who
could answer the phone and type. Today, entry-level clerical
workers need to know at least 2-3 types of software to do their job.
That wasn't the case even 10 years ago. Even certain manual-
labor jobs are going to require knowledge of technology in the
future."*

More Responsibility, More Education

The Society of Human Resource Management's (SHRM) 2002-2003
Workplace Forecast shows that only 27 percent of the U.S. population today
has a traditional four-year bachelor's degree, but that tomorrow's hottest
jobs will require *at least* a bachelor's.

All but two of the 50 highest-paying occupations of the future will
require a college degree, SHRM says. New jobs will increasingly require
both general and occupation-specific skills, will be more demanding, will
involve more teamwork, worker participation, and will be in occupations
that require people to think and be creative on the job.

This information is borne out by government figures. The U.S. Bureau of
Labor Statistics estimates that over the 2000-2010 period, total employment
will increase by 15 percent, but the service-producing sector will continue
to be the dominant employment generator, adding roughly 20 million jobs
by 2010 or an increase of 19 percent over that period. Meanwhile, manufacturing employment is expected to increase by only 3 percent over the 2000-
2010 period. In total, professional and service occupations are expected to
increase the fastest and to add the most jobs. Eight of the ten fastest
growing occupations are information technology occupations.

What Does That Mean When Selecting a Major?

No, this does not mean you should switch your major from culinary arts to computer engineering. You can still pursue your interests, whatever they are. You simply need to ask yourself the following questions about your choice of major:

- Does this major *at this particular school* offer coursework that prepares me for the latest technology and industry specific skills that I will encounter on the job?
- Does this major require coursework in composition and presentation skills?
- Is the general education required course work presented as a coherent package with a strong philosophy of educating the total person?
- Will this major and school provide me with internship or part-time employment opportunities that will build on-the-job skills that are attractive to employers?
- Does this major at this college give me an idea of what training I will need in the coming years to continue working in this field?
- Will I be building a strong foundation that will prepare me for further required study in this field?

Asking these important questions will help you select a major, as well as stay on course toward graduation. According to the National Association of Colleges and Employers' (NACE) 2003 Graduating Student & Alumni Survey, more than half of all undergraduates change their majors during their college careers—27 percent of undergraduates said they had changed their major once during their education, and nearly 24 percent said they had changed their major more than once.

It is significant that more than half of college graduates report a change in majors because:

- Changing majors indicates that students may not have researched their college and major alternatives well in the beginning
- They are likely to spend more on tuition and take longer to complete their degrees
- Future employers may find graduates lack key skills in information processing, communication, and critical thinking because they were too busy developing two or more specified skill sets as major choices

The Hudson Institute, an Indianapolis-based public policy think tank, has reported that the pace of technology is creating a severe skills gap in our country. The organization predicts that by 2020 there will be labor shortages in technical areas. At the same time, the U.S. Department of Labor has reported that new entrants into the workforce can expect to work for nine, yes nine, employers between the ages of 18-34.

This means that you will be doing a lot of training and re-training, either on your dime or your employer's. You may be selecting different majors as you move through the job market—so it is very important to have a solid education in the foundation course work as a first step.

Chapter Summary:

- Information processing skills will be required in every field. They are the perfect fit to go with a specialized major field of your choosing.
- Do not underestimate the value of a liberal arts education no matter what your career choice. It will give you the communications and thinking skills you need to be flexible in job choices throughout your working life.

SECTION 3

....

The Majors

CHAPTER 9

■■■■■■■■■■■■■■■■■■■

A CLOSER LOOK AT THE
213 MAJORS

The symbols you see below will accompany the 213 college majors you will review starting on page 85. They are just one more aid to give you more perspective on your choice—these symbols will appear next to each major where they apply. They will give you a convenient way to evaluate key traits that are shared by college major choices. You may also want to search the major listings to find those that have a specific trait that is important to you.

 Cultural Awareness—An opportunity to explore the world, its people, places, and opportunities

---

 Time Required to Get First Marketable Degree—The time to get a degree should be less than average

---

 Chance to Land a Job in Field—A high percentage of graduates land jobs in the field which they studied

---

 Preparation for Further Education—This major has more emphasis on building a foundation for further graduate school work

---

Information on 213 College Majors

A/V SYSTEMS

CLUSTER:

1 Applied Technology

WHERE TO SURF:

- National Association of Acoustical Consultants [www.ncac.com]
- The Architectural Engineering Institute [www.aeinstitute.org/default2.htm]
- American Institute of Architects [www.aia.org]

ACCOUNTING

CLUSTER:

#2 Computational

WHERE TO SURF:

- American Institute of Certified Public Accountants [www.aicpa.org]
- National Association of State Boards of Accountancy [www.nasba.org]
- Accreditation Council for Accountancy and Taxation [www.acatcredentials.org]

ACTUARIAL SCIENCE

CLUSTER:

#1 Applied Technology

WHERE TO SURF:

- Society of Actuaries (SOA) [www.soa.org]
- American Society of Pension Actuaries [www.aspa.org]
- Casualty Actuarial Society (CAS) [www.casact.org]

ADMINISTRATIVE ASSISTANT

CLUSTER:

#8 Verbal

WHERE TO SURF:

- National Association of Executive Secretaries and Administrative Assistants [www.naesaa.com]
- International Association of Administrative Professionals [www.iaap-hq.org]

AEROSPACE ENGINEERING

CLUSTER:

#1 Applied Technology

WHERE TO SURF:

- American Institute of Aeronautics and Astronautics [www.aiaa.org]
- Junior Engineering Technical Society [www.jets.org]
- Aerospace Industries Association [www.aia-aerospace.org]

AFRICAN AMERICAN STUDIES

CLUSTER:

#5 Social Sciences

WHERE TO SURF:

- Association for the Study of African American Life and History [www.asalh.com]
- National Association of African American Studies [www.naaas.org]
- National Council for Black Studies [www.nationalcouncilforblackstudies.com]

AGRICULTURE

CLUSTER:

#1 Applied Technology

WHERE TO SURF:

- American Society of Agricultural Engineers [www.asae.org]

AMERICAN STUDIES

CLUSTER:

#5 Social Sciences

WHERE TO SURF:

- American Studies Association [www.Georgetown.edu/crossroads/asainfo.html]

ANATOMY

CLUSTER:

#3 Science-Related

WHERE TO SURF:

- Case Western Reserve School of Medicine [www.cwru.edu]

ANIMATION
CLUSTER:

#10 Technical Arts

WHERE TO SURF:

• International Animation Association [www.swcp.com/animate]

ANTHROPOLOGY
CLUSTER:

#3 Science-Related

WHERE TO SURF:

• American Anthropological Association [www.aaanet.org]

ARCHAEOLOGY
CLUSTER:

#3 Science-Related

WHERE TO SURF:

• Society for American Archaeology [www.saa.org]
• Archaeological Institute of America [www.archaeological.org]

ARCHITECTURAL ENGINEERING
CLUSTER:

#1 Applied Technology

WHERE TO SURF:

• The Architectural Engineering Institute [www.aeinstitute.org]
• American Institute of Architects [www.aia.org/conted/default.asp]

ARCHITECTURE
CLUSTER:

#1 Applied Technology

WHERE TO SURF:

• American Institute of Architects [www.aia.org]
• National Council of Architectural Registration Boards [www.ncarb.org]

ART
CLUSTER:

#9 Fine/Professional Art

WHERE TO SURF:

• National Association of Schools of Art and Design
[http://nasad.arts-accredit.org]

ART [Fine Art]...

CLUSTER:

#9 Fine/Professional Art

WHERE TO SURF:

• National Association of Schools of Art and Design
[http://nasad.arts-accredit.org]

ART AND DESIGN ....

CLUSTER:

#9 Fine/Professional Art

WHERE TO SURF:

• National Association of Schools of Art and Design
[http://nasad.arts-accredit.org]

ART HISTORY ....

CLUSTER:

#9 Fine/Professional Art

WHERE TO SURF:

• Society of American Archivists [www.archivists.org

• American Association of Museums [www.aam-us.org]

ART PRE-PROFESSIONAL ....

CLUSTER:

#9 Fine/Professional Art

WHERE TO SURF:

• National Association of Schools of Art and Design
[http://nasad.arts-accredit.org]

ART THERAPY ....

CLUSTER:

#3 Social Sciences

WHERE TO SURF:

• American Therapeutic Recreation Association
[www.atra-online.org]

ARTS AND LETTERS GENERAL

CLUSTER:

#7 Language

WHERE TO SURF:

• Resources of Scholarly Societies
[www. scholarly-societies.org/genartshumanities_soc.html]

ASIAN STUDIES

CLUSTER:

#5 Social Sciences

WHERE TO SURF:

• Association for Asian Studies [www.aasianst.org]

ASTRONOMY

CLUSTER:

#3 Science-Related

WHERE TO SURF:

• Association of Universities for Research in Astronomy
[www.aura-astronomy.org]

ATHLETIC TRAINING

CLUSTER:

#4 Allied Health

WHERE TO SURF:

• National Athletic Trainers Association [www.nata.org]

• American Medical Association [www.ama-assn.org]

BIOCHEMISTRY

CLUSTER:

#3 Science-Related

WHERE TO SURF:

• Federation of American Societies for Experimental Biology
[www.faseb.org]

• American Institute of Biological Sciences [www.aibs.org]

BIOLOGY

CLUSTER:

#3 Science-Related

WHERE TO SURF:

• American Institute of Biological Sciences [www.aibs.org]

BIOMEDICAL ENGINEERING

CLUSTER:

#3 Science-Related

WHERE TO SURF:

• Biomedical Engineering Society [www.bmes.org]

BOTANY

CLUSTER:

#3 Science-Related

WHERE TO SURF:

• Botanical Society of America [www.botany.org]

BROADCASTING

CLUSTER:

#10 Technical Arts

WHERE TO SURF:

• North American Broadcasters Association [www.nabanet.com/wbuArea/members/about.asp]

BUSINESS ADMINISTRATION

CLUSTER:

#2 Computational

WHERE TO SURF:

• American Management Association [www.amanet.org]

• National Management Association [www.nma1.org]

CARDIOVASCULAR TECHNOLOGY

CLUSTER:

#4 Allied Health

WHERE TO SURF:

• Alliance of Cardiovascular Professionals [www.acp-online.org]

• Committee on Accreditation for Allied Health Education Programs [www.caahep.org]

CARTOGRAPHY/SURVEYING

CLUSTER:

#1 Applied Technology

WHERE TO SURF:

• National Society of Professional Surveyors [www.acsm.net]

• ASPRS: The Imaging and Geospatial Information Society [www.asprs.org]

CHEMICAL ENGINEERING

CLUSTER:

#1 Applied Technology

WHERE TO SURF:

• American Institute of Chemical Engineers [www.aiche.org]

CHEMISTRY

CLUSTER:

#4 Science-Related

WHERE TO SURF:

• American Chemical Society, Education Division [www.acs.org]

CHILDCARE STUDIES

CLUSTER:

#6 Human Services

WHERE TO SURF:

• National Association for the Education of Young Children [http://naeyc.org/]

• National Childcare Association [www.nccanet.org]

CHIROPRACTIC

CLUSTER:

#3 Science-Related

WHERE TO SURF:

• American Chiropractic Association [www.amerchiro.org]

• International Chiropractors Association [www.chiropractic.org]

CIVIL ENGINEERING ....

CLUSTER:

#1 Applied Technology

WHERE TO SURF:

• American Society of Civil Engineers [www.asce.org]

CLASSICAL LANGUAGES - GREEK..

CLUSTER:

#7 Language

WHERE TO SURF:

• Modern Greek Studies Association [http://mgs.cla.umn.edu]

CLASSICAL LANGUAGES - LATIN ....

CLUSTER:

#7 Language

WHERE TO SURF:

• The Later Latin Society [www.informalmusic.com/latinsoc]

COACHING ....

CLUSTER:

#6 Human Services

WHERE TO SURF:

• National High School Coaches Association [www.nhsca.com]

COMPUTER AIDED DRAFTING ....

CLUSTER:

#1 Applied Technology

WHERE TO SURF:

• American Design Drafting Association [www.adda.org]

• Commission of Career Schools and Colleges of Technology
[www.accsct.org]

COMPUTER APPLICATIONS...

CLUSTER:

#1 Applied Technology, #2 Computational

WHERE TO SURF:

• Institute for Certification of Computing Professionals [www.iccp.org]

• Association for Computing Machinery [www.acm.org]

COMPUTER MAINTENANCE

CLUSTER:

#1 Applied Technology

WHERE TO SURF:

- Association of Computer Support Specialists [www.acss.org]
- Association of Support Professionals [www.sage.org]
- National Workforce Center for Emerging Technologies [ww.nwcet.org]

COMPUTER NETWORKS

CLUSTER:

#1 Applied Technology,

#2 Computational

WHERE TO SURF:

- Network Professional Association [www.npanet.org]

COMPUTER PROGRAMMING

CLUSTER:

#1 Applied Technology

WHERE TO SURF:

- Institute for Certification of Computing Professionals [www.iccp.org]
- Association for Computing Machinery [www.acm.org]

COMPUTER SCIENCE

CLUSTER:

#1 Applied Technology

WHERE TO SURF:

- IEEE Computer Society [www.computer.org]
- Association of Computer Support Specialists [www.acss.org]
- Association of Support Professionals [www.sage.org]
- National Workforce Center for Emerging Technologies [www.nwcet.org]

COMPUTER STUDIES

CLUSTER:

#1 Applied Technology

WHERE TO SURF:

- Commission of Career Schools and Colleges of Technology [www.accsct.org]
- American Electronics Association [www.aeanet.org]
- Institute for Certification of Computing Professionals [www.iccp.org]

COMPUTER SYSTEMS ....

CLUSTER:

#2 Computational

WHERE TO SURF:

• Association for Computing Machinery [www.acm.org]

• Institute of Electrical and Electronics Engineers Computer Society [www.computer.org]

CONSTRUCTION TECHNOLOGY ....

CLUSTER:

#1 Applied Technology

WHERE TO SURF:

• Building Trades Directory [www.buildingtradesdir.com]

COSMETOLOGY ....

CLUSTER:

#10 Technical Arts

WHERE TO SURF:

• National Accrediting Commission of Cosmetology Arts and Sciences [www.naccas.org]

• National Cosmetology Association [www.salonprofessionals.org]

COUNSELING ....

CLUSTER:

#5 Social Sciences

#6 Human Services

WHERE TO SURF:

• American Counseling Association [www.counseling.org]

• National Board for Certified Counselors, Inc. [www.nbcc.org]

COURT REPORTING ....

CLUSTER:

8 Verbal

WHERE TO SURF:

• National Court Reporters Association [www.ncraonline.org]

• United States Court Reporters Association [www.uscra.org]

• National Verbatim Reporters Association [www.nvra.org]

CREATIVE WRITING

CLUSTER:

#10 Fine/Professional Art

WHERE TO SURF:

- Association of American Publishers [www.publishers.org]
- Graphic Communications Council [www.npes.org]
- Graphic Arts Technical Foundation [www.gatf.org]
- American Book Publishers Association [www.publishers.org]

CRIMINAL JUSTICE AND ADMINISTRATION

CLUSTER:

#2 Computational

WHERE TO SURF:

- Federal Bureau of Investigation [www.fbi.gov]
- National Center for State Courts [www.ncsonline.org]

CRIMINOLOGY

CLUSTER:

#6 Human Services

WHERE TO SURF:

- American Society of Criminology [www.asc41.com]
- American Sociological Association [www.assanet.org]

CULINARY ARTS

CLUSTER:

#10 Technical Arts

WHERE TO SURF:

- National Restaurant Association [www.restaurant.org]
- American Culinary Federation [www.acfchefs.org]
- International Council on Hotel, Restaurant, and Institutional Education [http://www.chrie.org]

DANCE

CLUSTER:

#9 Fine/Professional Art

WHERE TO SURF:

- National Association of Schools of Dance [nasd.arts-accredit.org]
- Dance USA [www.danceusa.org]
- Screen Actors Guild [www.sag.org]
- American Federation of Television and Radio Artists [www.aftra.org]

DATABASE MANAGEMENT

CLUSTER:

#2 Computational

WHERE TO SURF:

- Institute of Electrical and Electronics Engineers Computer Society [www.computer.org]
- National Workforce Center for Emerging Technologies [www.nwcet.org]

DATABASE PROGRAMMING

CLUSTER:

#2 Computational

WHERE TO SURF:

- Association for Computing Machinery [www.acm.org]
- Institute of Electrical and Electronics Engineers Computer Society [www.computer.org]
- National Workforce Center for Emerging Technologies [www.nwcet.org]

DECISION SUPPORT SYSTEMS

CLUSTER:

#1 Applied Technology

WHERE TO SURF:

- IEEE Computer Society [www.computer.org]
- National Workforce Center for Emerging Technologies [www.nwcet.org]
- Association of Information Technology Professionals [www.aitp.org/index.jsp]

DENTAL ASSISTING

CLUSTER:

#4 Allied Health

#6 Human Services

WHERE TO SURF:

• Commission on Dental Accreditation, American Dental Association [www.ada.org]

DENTAL HYGIENE

CLUSTER:

#4 Allied Health

WHERE TO SURF:

• American Dental Hygienists' Association [www.adha.org]

• Commission on Dental Accreditation, American Dental Association [www.ada.org]

DENTISTRY

CLUSTER:

#3 Science-Related

WHERE TO SURF:

• American Dental Association [www.ada.org]

DIGITAL MEDIA TECHNOLOGY

CLUSTER:

#10 Fine/Professional Art

WHERE TO SURF:

• The National Association of Schools of Art and Design [www.arts-accredit.org/nasad/default.htm]

• Women in Animation [www.womeninanimation.org]

DRUG REHABILITATION

CLUSTER:

#6 Human Services

WHERE TO SURF:

• American Counseling Association [www.counseling.org]

EARTH SCIENCE

CLUSTER:

#3 Science-Related

WHERE TO SURF:

• American Geological Institute [www.agiweb.org]

ECOLOGY

CLUSTER:

#3 Science-Related

WHERE TO SURF:

• American Geological Institute [ww.agiweb.org]

• American Association of Petroleum Geologists [www.aapg.org]

ECONOMICS

CLUSTER:

#2 Computational

WHERE TO SURF:

• National Association for Business Economics [www.nabe.com]

• American Economic Association [www.Vanderbilt.edu/AEA/]

EDUCATION [Elementary]

CLUSTER:

#6 Human Services

WHERE TO SURF:

• National Council for Accreditation of Teacher Education [www.ncate.org]

• National Association for the Education of Young Children [www.naeyc.org]

EDUCATION [Music]

CLUSTER:

#6 Human Services

WHERE TO SURF:

• National Association for Music Education [www.menc.org]

EDUCATION [Secondary]

CLUSTER:

#6 Human Services

WHERE TO SURF:

• Recruiting New Teachers [www.rnt.org]

EDUCATION [Special Education]

CLUSTER:

#6 Human Services

WHERE TO SURF:

• National Clearinghouse for Professions in Special Education, Council for Exceptional Children [www.special-ed-careers.org]

EDUCATION [Teacher Aides/Assistants]

CLUSTER:

#6 Human Services

WHERE TO SURF:

• U.S. Department of Labor Bureau of Labor Statistics [stats.bls.gov/oco/ocos153.htm]

EEG TECHNOLOGY

CLUSTER:

#4 Allied Health

WHERE TO SURF:

• College Board [www.collegeboard.com]

ELECTRICAL & COMPUTER ENGINEERING

CLUSTER:

#1 Applied Technology

WHERE TO SURF:

• IEEE Computer Society [www.computer.org]

ELECTRICAL ENGINEERING

CLUSTER:

#1 Applied Technology

WHERE TO SURF:

• JETS-Guidance [www.jets.org]

• Accreditation Board for Engineering and Technology, Inc. [www.abet.org]

ENGINEERING TECHNOLOGY...

CLUSTER:

#1 Applied Technology

WHERE TO SURF:

- JETS-Guidance, [www.jets.org]
- Accreditation Board for Engineering and Technology [www.abet.org]
- National Institute for Certification in Engineering Technologies [www.nicet.org]

ENGLISH LITERATURE...

CLUSTER:

#7 Language

WHERE TO SURF:

- English Literature on the Web [www.lang.nagoya-u.ac.jp/~matsuoka/EngLit.html]

ENVIRONMENT CONTROL TECHNOLOGY ....

CLUSTER:

#1 Applied Technology

WHERE TO SURF:

- Refrigeration Service Engineers Society [www.rses.org]
- Plumbing-Heating-Cooling Contractors [www.phccweb.org]
- North American Technician Excellence [www.natex.org]
- Home Builders Institute [www.hbi.org]
- Mechanical Contractors Association of America [www.mcaa.org]
- Air-Conditioning and Refrigeration Institute [www.ari.org]

ENVIRONMENT DESIGN ....

CLUSTER:

#1 Applied Technology

#2 Computational

WHERE TO SURF:

- National Association of Schools of Art and Design [http://nasad.arts-accredit.org]

ENVIRONMENTAL ENGINEERING

CLUSTER:

#1 Applied Technology

WHERE TO SURF:

- American Academy of Environmental Engineers [www.aaee.net]

ENVIRONMENTAL HEALTH ENGINEERING

CLUSTER:

#1 Applied Technology

WHERE TO SURF:

- American Academy of Environmental Engineers [www.aaee.net]

FAMILY COUNSELING

CLUSTER:

#5 Social Sciences

WHERE TO SURF:

- American Counseling Association [www.counseling.org]
- National Board for Certified Counselors, Inc. [www.nbcc.org]

FASHION DESIGN

CLUSTER:

#10 Technical Arts

WHERE TO SURF:

- National Association of Schools of Art and Design [www.arts-accredit.org/nasad/default.htm]

FASHION MERCHANDISING

CLUSTER:

#10 Technical Arts

WHERE TO SURF:

- Institute for Supply Management [www.ism.ws]
- National Institute of Governmental Purchasing [www.nigp.org]

FILM STUDY

CLUSTER:

#9 Fine/Professional Art

WHERE TO SURF:

- Directors Guild of America [www.dga.org]
- Screen Actors Guild [www.sag.org]
- Producers Guild of America [www.producersguild.org]

FILM/TV

CLUSTER:

#9 Fine/Professional Art

WHERE TO SURF:

- Directors Guild of America [www.dga.org]
- Screen Actors Guild [www.sag.org]
- Producers Guild of America [www.producersguild.org]

FINANCE

CLUSTER:

#2 Computational

WHERE TO SURF:

- Association for Financial Professionals [www.afponline.org]
- American Bankers Association [www.aba.com]

FITNESS SPECIALIST

CLUSTER:

#4 Allied Health

#6 Human Services

WHERE TO SURF:

- American Council on Exercise [www.acefitness.org]

FORENSIC SCIENCE

CLUSTER:

#3 Science-Related

WHERE TO SURF:

- American Academy of Forensic Sciences [www.aafs.org]

FORESTRY

CLUSTER:

#3 Science-Related

WHERE TO SURF:

- Forest Resources Association [www.forestresources.org]
- Northeastern Loggers Association [www.afandpa.org]

GENERAL SCIENCE

CLUSTER:

#3 Science-Related

WHERE TO SURF:

- American Association for the Advancement of Science [www.aaas.org]

GENERAL STUDIES

CLUSTER:

#5 Social Sciences

WHERE TO SURF:

- International Political Science Association [www.ipsa.ca]

GEOGRAPHY

CLUSTER:

#5 Social Sciences

WHERE TO SURF:

- Association of American Geographers [www.aag.org]

GEOLOGY

CLUSTER:

#3 Science-Related

WHERE TO SURF:

- American Geological Institute [www.agiweb.org]
- Geological Society of America [www.geosociety.org]
- American Association of Petroleum Geologists [www.aapg.org]

GOVERNMENT

CLUSTER:

#5 Social Sciences

WHERE TO SURF:

• College Board [www.collegeboard.com]

GRAPHIC ARTS AND DESIGN

CLUSTER:

#10 Technical Arts

WHERE TO SURF:

• American Institute of Graphic Arts [www.aiga.org]

• National Association of Schools of Art and Design [www.arts-accredit/nasad/default.htm]

HEALTH ASSISTANT

CLUSTER:

#4 Allied Health

WHERE TO SURF:

• Association of Family Practice Physician Assistants [www.afppa.org]

HEALTH INFORMATION TECHNOLOGY

CLUSTER:

#8 Verbal

WHERE TO SURF:

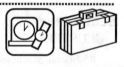

• American Health Information Management Association [www.ahima.org]

HEALTH SCIENCE

CLUSTER:

#3 Science-Related

WHERE TO SURF:

• American Association of Medical Assistants [www.aama-ntl.org]

• National Association of Emergency Medical Technicians [www.naemt.org]

HEALTHCARE MANAGEMENT ....

CLUSTER:

#2 Computational

WHERE TO SURF:

- Association of University Programs in Health Administration [www.aupha.org]
- Accrediting Commission on Education for Health Services Administration [www.acehsa.org]
- American College of Health Care Administrators [www.achca.org]

HEATING AND AIR CONDITIONING TECHNOLOGY ....

CLUSTER:

#1 Applied Technology

WHERE TO SURF:

- Air Conditioning Contractors of America [www.theaha.org]
- Sheet Metal and Air Conditioning Contractors' National Association [www.smacna.org]

HISTORY ....

CLUSTER:

#5 Social Sciences

WHERE TO SURF:

- American Historical Association [www.theaha.org]
- Organization of American Historians [www.oah.org]
- American Association for State and Local History [www.aaslh.org]

HISTORY AND PHILOSOPHY OF SCIENCE ....

CLUSTER:

#5 Social Sciences

WHERE TO SURF:

- American Historical Association [www.theaha.org]

HOME ECONOMICS ....

CLUSTER:

#2 Computational

WHERE TO SURF:

- American Association of Family and Consumer Sciences [www.aafcs.org]

HORTICULTURAL SCIENCE

CLUSTER:

#10 Technical Arts

WHERE TO SURF:

• American Horticultural Society [www.ahs.org]

HOSPITALITY AND RECREATION

CLUSTER:

#6 Human Services

WHERE TO SURF:

• American Hotel and Lodging Association [www.ahma.com]

• National Restaurant Association [www.restaurant.org]

HOSPITALITY MANAGEMENT

CLUSTER:

#6 Human Services

WHERE TO SURF:

• National Restaurant Association Educational Foundation [www.nraef.org]

• The International Council on Hotel, Restaurant, and Institutional Education [www.chrie.org]

HOTEL MANAGEMENT

CLUSTER:

#2 Computational

WHERE TO SURF:

• American Hotel and Lodging Association [www.ahma.com]

• National Restaurant Association [www.restaurant.org]

HUMAN RESOURCES

CLUSTER:

#6 Human Services

WHERE TO SURF:

• Society for Human Resource Management [www.shrm.org]

• American Society for Training and Development [www.astd.org]

INDUSTRIAL DESIGN

CLUSTER:

#1 Applied Technology

WHERE TO SURF:

• Industrial Designers Society of America [www.idsa.org]

INDUSTRIAL ENGINEERING

CLUSTER:

#1 Applied Technology

WHERE TO SURF:

• Institute of Industrial Engineers, Inc. [www.iienet.org]

INSTITUTIONAL ADMINISTRATION

CLUSTER:

#2 Computational

WHERE TO SURF:

• National Center on Nonprofit Enterprise [www.nationalcne.org]

INTERIOR DESIGN

CLUSTER:

#10 Technical Arts

WHERE TO SURF:

• International Interior Design Association [www.iida.org]
• American Society of Interior Designers [www.asid.org]

INTERNATIONAL BUSINESS

CLUSTER:

#2 Computational

WHERE TO SURF:

• Financial Executives International [www.fei.org]
• American Management Association [www.amanet.org]

INTERNATIONAL STUDIES

CLUSTER:

#2 Computational

WHERE TO SURF:

• Foreign Policy Association [www.fpa.org]
• Council on Foreign Relations [www.cfr.org]

JEWISH STUDIES

CLUSTER:

#5 Social Sciences

WHERE TO SURF:

- Rabbinical Council of America [www.rabbis.org]
- Jewish Theological Seminary of America [www.itsa.edu]
- Hebrew Union College-Jewish Institute of Religion [www.huc.edu]
- Reconstructionist Rabbinical College [www.rrc.edu]

JOURNALISM

CLUSTER:

#8 Verbal

WHERE TO SURF:

- National Association of Broadcasters [www.nab.org]
- Accrediting Council on Education in Journalism and
  Mass Communications, University of Kansas School of Journalism
  and Mass Communications
  [www2.ku.edu/~acejmc]

LANDSCAPING

CLUSTER:

#10 Technical Arts

WHERE TO SURF:

- American Nursery and Landscape Association
  [www.anla.org]

LAW

CLUSTER:

#2 Computational

#8 Verbal

WHERE TO SURF:

- American Bar Association [www.abanet.org]
- Law School Admission Council [www.isac.org]

LAW - PARALEGAL STUDIES

CLUSTER:

#8 Verbal

WHERE TO SURF:

- Standing Committee on Legal Assistants, American Bar Association [www.abanet.org]

LAW ENFORCEMENT

CLUSTER:

#6 Human Services

WHERE TO SURF:

- The Federal Law Enforcement Officers Association [www.fleoa.org]

LIBRARY SCIENCE

CLUSTER:

#8 Verbal

WHERE TO SURF:

- American Library Association [www.ala.org]
- Special Libraries Association [www.sla.org]
- Association for Library and Information Science Education [www.alise.org]

LINGUISTICS

CLUSTER:

#7 Language

WHERE TO SURF:

- International Quantitative Linguistics Association [www.iqla.org]

MANAGEMENT

CLUSTER:

#2 Computational

WHERE TO SURF:

- American Management Association [www.amanet.org/index.htm]

MANAGEMENT INFORMATION SYSTEMS

CLUSTER:

#1 Applied Technology

WHERE TO SURF:

• National Workforce Center for Emerging Technologies [www.nwcet.org]

MARKETING

CLUSTER:

#2 Computational

WHERE TO SURF:

• American Marketing Association [www.marketingpower.com]

MASSAGE THERAPY

CLUSTER:

#4 Allied Health

#6 Human Services

WHERE TO SURF:

• American Massage Therapy Association [www.amtamassage.org/]

MATERIAL SCIENCE ENGINEERING

CLUSTER:

#1 Applied Technology

WHERE TO SURF:

• The Minerals, Metals, & Materials Society [www.tms.org]
• ASM International [www.asm-intl.org]
• American Mathematical Society [www.ams.org]
• Society for Industrial and Applied Mathematics [www.siam.org/alterindex.htm]

MATH AND COMPUTER SCIENCE

CLUSTER:

#1 Applied Technology

WHERE TO SURF:

• American Mathematical Society [www.ams.org]
• Society for Industrial and Applied Mathematics [www.siam.org]

MECHANICAL DRAFTING

CLUSTER:

#1 Applied Technology

WHERE TO SURF:

- American Design Drafting Association [www.adda.org]

MECHANICAL ENGINEERING

CLUSTER:

#1 Applied Technology

WHERE TO SURF:

- The American Society of Mechanical Engineers [www.asme.org]

MEDIA ARTS

CLUSTER:

#10 Technical Arts

WHERE TO SURF:

- National Alliance for Media Arts and Culture [www.namac.org]
- International Digital Media Arts Association [www.idmaa.org]

MEDICAL ADMINISTRATION

CLUSTER:

#4 Allied Health

WHERE TO SURF:

- American Medial Technologists [www.amt1.com]

MEDICAL ASSISTING

CLUSTER:

#4 Allied Health

WHERE TO SURF:

- American Association of Medical Assistants
  [www.aama-ntl.org]

MEDICAL RECORDS

CLUSTER:

#4 Allied Health

WHERE TO SURF:

- American Health Information Management Association
  [www.ahima.org]

MEDICINE
CLUSTER:

#3 Science-Related

WHERE TO SURF:

• American Medical Association [www.assn.org]

• American College of Surgeons [www.facs.org]

MEDIEVAL STUDIES
CLUSTER:

#5 Social Sciences

WHERE TO SURF:

• Harvard University [www.fas.Harvard.edu/~medieval]

METALLURGICAL ENGINEERING
CLUSTER:

#1 Applied Technology

WHERE TO SURF:

• Minerals, Metals, & Materials Society [www.tms.org];

• ASM International Foundation [www.asm-intl.org]

METEOROLOGY
CLUSTER:

#1 Applied Technology

WHERE TO SURF:

• American Meteorological Society [www.ametsoc.org/AMS]

MICROBIOLOGY
CLUSTER:

#3 Science-Related

WHERE TO SURF:

• American Society for Microbiology [www.asmusa.org]

MILITARY SCIENCE

CLUSTER:

#1 Applied Technology

WHERE TO SURF:

- U.S. Army [www.army.mil]
- U.S. Air Force [www.af.mil]
- U.S. Marines [www.usmc.mil]
- U.S. Navy [www.navy.mil]

MINING ENGINEERING

CLUSTER:

#1 Applied Technology

WHERE TO SURF:

- Michigan Technological University [www.mfu.edu]
- The Society for Mining, Metallurgy and Exploration [www.smenet.org]
- National Workforce Center for Emerging Technologies [www.nwcet.org]

MODERN AND CLASSICAL LANGUAGE

CLUSTER:

#7 Language

WHERE TO SURF:

- American Classical League [www.aclclassics.org]

MODERN LANGUAGES - ARABIC

CLUSTER:

#7 Language

WHERE TO SURF:

- Georgetown University Department of Arabic Language, Literature and Linguistics [www.georgetown.edu/departments/arabic/]

MODERN LANGUAGES - CHINESE

CLUSTER:

#7 Language

WHERE TO SURF:

- Chinese Language Teachers Association, Inc. [clta-us.org]

MODERN LANGUAGES - FRENCH ....

CLUSTER:

#7 Language

WHERE TO SURF:

• Association for French Language Studies
[www.afls.net]

MODERN LANGUAGES - GERMAN ....

CLUSTER:

#7 Language

WHERE TO SURF:

• Association for Language Learning
[www.all-languages.org.uk]

MODERN LANGUAGES - ITALIAN ....

CLUSTER:

#7 Language

WHERE TO SURF:

• Association for Language Learning
[www.all-languages.org.uk]

MODERN LANGUAGES - RUSSIAN...

CLUSTER:

#7 Language

WHERE TO SURF:

• Association for Language Learning
[www.all-languages.org.uk]

MODERN LANGUAGES - SPANISH ....

CLUSTER:

#7 Language

WHERE TO SURF:

• Association for Language Learning
[www.all-languages.org.uk]

MUSIC COMPOSITION

CLUSTER:

#9 Fine/Professional Art

WHERE TO SURF:

• National Association of Schools of Music
[nasm.arts-accredit.org]

MUSIC EDUCATION

CLUSTER:

#9 Fine/Professional Art

#10 Technical Arts

WHERE TO SURF:

• National Association for Music Education
[www.menc.org]

MUSIC INSTRUMENTAL

CLUSTER:

#9 Fine/Professional Art

WHERE TO SURF:

• National Association of Schools of Music
[nasm.arts-accredit.org]

MUSIC VOCAL

CLUSTER:

#9 Fine/Professional Art

WHERE TO SURF:

• National Association of Schools of Music
[nasm.arts-accredit.org]

NATURAL SCIENCE

CLUSTER:

#3 Science-Related

WHERE TO SURF:

• Scholarly Societies Project
[www.lib.uwaterloo.ca/society/earthsci_soc.html]

NAVAL SCIENCE

CLUSTER:

#1 Applied Technology

WHERE TO SURF:

- The Association of Scientists and Engineers of the Naval Sea Systems Command [www.navsea.navy.mil]

NETWORK ADMINISTRATION

CLUSTER:

#1 Applied Technology

WHERE TO SURF:

- Association of Computer Support Specialists [www.acss.org]

- System Administrators Guild [www.sage.org]

NETWORK MANAGEMENT

CLUSTER:

#1 Applied Technology

WHERE TO SURF:

- National Workforce Center for Emerging Technologies [www.nwcet.org]

- Network Professional Association [www.npanet.org]

NUCLEAR ENGINEERING

CLUSTER:

#1 Applied Technology

WHERE TO SURF:

- American Nuclear Society [www.ans.org]

NUCLEAR MEDICINE

CLUSTER:

#4 Allied Health

WHERE TO SURF:

- Society of Nuclear Medicine Technologists [www.snm.org]

NURSING

CLUSTER:

#4 Allied Health

WHERE TO SURF:

- National League for Nursing [www.nln.org]
- American Association of Colleges of Nursing [www.aacn.nche.edu]
- American Nurses Association [www.nursingworld.org]

OCCUPATIONAL THERAPY

CLUSTER:

#4 Allied Health

WHERE TO SURF:

- The American Occupational Therapy Association [www.aota.org]

OCCUPATIONAL THERAPY ASSISTING

CLUSTER:

#4 Allied Health

WHERE TO SURF:

- American Occupational Therapy Association [www.aota.org]

OCEANOGRAPHY

CLUSTER:

#3 Science-Related

WHERE TO SURF:

- Marine Technology Society [www.mtsociety.org]

OPTHALMIC LABORATORY TECHNOLOGY

CLUSTER:

#4 Allied Health

WHERE TO SURF:

- Opticians Association of America [www.oaa.org]

OPTOMETRY ....

CLUSTER:

#3 Science-Related

WHERE TO SURF:

- Association of Schools and Colleges of Optometry [www.opted.org]
- American Optometric Association, Educational Services [www.aoanet.org]

ORGANIZATIONAL STUDIES ....

CLUSTER:

#6 Human Services

WHERE TO SURF:

- American Psychological Association [www.apa.org]
- National Association of School Psychologists [www.nasponline.org]
- Association of State and Provincial Psychology Boards [www.asppb.org]
- American Board of Professional Psychology [www.abpp.org]

PETROLEUM ENGINEERING ....

CLUSTER:

#1 Applied Technology

WHERE TO SURF:

- Society of Petroleum Engineers [www.spe.org]

PHARMACY..

CLUSTER:

#3 Science-Related

WHERE TO SURF:

- American Association of Colleges of Pharmacy [www.aacp.org]
- National Association of Boards of Pharmacy [www.nabp.net]
- National Association of Chain Drug Stores [www.nacds.org]

PHARMACY TECHNOLOGY ....

CLUSTER:

#3 Science Related

WHERE TO SURF:

- Pharmacy Technician Certification Board [www.ptcb.org]

PHILOSOPHY

CLUSTER:

#5 Social Sciences

WHERE TO SURF:

- American Philosophical Association [www.udel.edu/apa]

PHYSICAL EDUCATION

CLUSTER:

#4 Allied Health

WHERE TO SURF:

- American Alliance for Health Physical Education Recreation and Dance [www.aahperd.org]
- National Recreation and Park Association [www.activeparks.org]
- American Council on Exercise [www.acefitness.org]
- American College of Sports Medicine [www.acsm.org]
- National Strength and Conditioning Association [www.nsca-lift.org]

PHYSICAL SCIENCE

CLUSTER:

#3 Science-Related

WHERE TO SURF:

- Scholarly Societies Project [www.lib.uwaterloo.ca/society]

PHYSICAL THERAPY

CLUSTER:

#4 Allied Health

WHERE TO SURF:

- American Physical Therapy Association [www.apta.org]

PHYSICAL TRAINING

CLUSTER:

#4 Allied Health

WHERE TO SURF:

- The American Physical Therapy Association [www.apta.org]
- American Council on Exercise [www.acefitness.org]
- American College of Sports Medicine [www.acsm.org]
- National Strength and Conditioning Association [www.nsca-lift.org]

PHYSICS

CLUSTER:

#3 Science-Related

WHERE TO SURF:

- American Institute of Physics [www.aip.org]
- American Physical Society [www.aps.org]

PODIATRY

CLUSTER:

#3 Science-Related

WHERE TO SURF:

- American Podiatric Medical Association [www.apma.org]
- American Association of Colleges of Podiatric Medicine [www.aacpm.org]

POLITICAL SCIENCE

CLUSTER:

#3 Social Sciences

WHERE TO SURF:

- National Association of Schools of Public Affairs and Administration [www.naspaa.org]

PRACTICAL NURSE (LPN)

CLUSTER:

#4 Allied Health

#6 Human Services

WHERE TO SURF:

- American Nurses Association [www.nursingworld.org]
- American Association of Colleges of Nursing [www.aacn.nche.edu]

PSYCHIATRIC SOCIAL WORK

CLUSTER:

#6 Human Services

WHERE TO SURF:

- National Association of Social Workers [www.naswdc.org]
- Council on Social Work Education [www.cswe.org]
- Association of Social Work Boards [www.aswb.org]

PSYCHOLOGY

CLUSTER:

#5 Social Sciences

WHERE TO SURF:

- American Psychological Association [www.apa.org]
- National Association of School Psychologists [www.nasponline.org]

PUBLISHING

CLUSTER:

#8 Verbal

WHERE TO SURF:

- Association of American Publishers [www.publishers.org]
- Acoustical Society of America [http://asa.aip.org/index.html]
- Society of Motion Picture and Television Engineers [www.smpte.org]

RADIOLOGY TECHNOLOGY

CLUSTER:

#4 Allied Health

WHERE TO SURF:

- American Society of Radiologic Technologists [www.asrt.org]

REAL ESTATE

CLUSTER:

#2 Computational

#8 Verbal

WHERE TO SURF

- National Association of Realtors [www.realtor.com]

RECORDS MANAGEMENT

CLUSTER:

#2 Computational

#8 Verbal

WHERE TO SURF

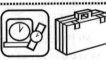

- ARMA International [www.arma.org]

RECREATIONAL THERAPY

CLUSTER:

#4 Allied Health

WHERE TO SURF:

- American Therapeutic Recreation Association
  [www.atra-tr.org]
- National Council for Therapeutic Recreation Certification
  [www.nctrc.org]

RELIGION/THEOLOGY

CLUSTER:

#5 Social Sciences

WHERE TO SURF:

- College Board [www.collegeboard.com]

RESPIRATORY THERAPY

CLUSTER:

#4 Allied Health

WHERE TO SURF:

- American Association for Respiratory Care
  [www.aarc.org]
- National Board for Respiratory Care [www.nbrc.org]

SCULPTING

CLUSTER:

#9 Fine/Professional Art

WHERE TO SURF:

- Sculptor.org [www.sculptor.org]

SECURITY SYSTEMS

CLUSTER:

#1 Applied Technology

WHERE TO SURF:

- SUNY [www.sunytccc.edu/academic/forensic/main.asp]

SOCIAL WORK ....

CLUSTER:

#5 Social Sciences

#6 Human Services

WHERE TO SURF:

- National Association of Social Workers [www.socialworkers.org]
- Council on Social Work Education [www.cswe.org]

SOCIAL WORK ASSISTANT ....

CLUSTER:

#6 Human Services

WHERE TO SURF:

- National Organization for Human Service Education [www.nohse.org]
- Council for Standards in Human Services Education, Harrisburg Area Community College, Human Services Program [www.cshse.org]

SOCIOLOGY ....

CLUSTER:

#5 Social Sciences

WHERE TO SURF:

- American Sociological Association [www.asanet.org]

SONOGRAPHY ....

CLUSTER:

#4 Allied Health

WHERE TO SURF:

- Society of Diagnostic Medical Sonography [www.sdms.org]
- American Registry of Diagnostic Medical Sonographers [www.ardms.org]
- Joint Review Committee on Education in Diagnostic Medical Sonography [www.caahep.org]

SPEECH & DRAMA

CLUSTER:

#9 Fine/Professional Art

WHERE TO SURF:

- National Association of Dramatic and Speech Arts, Inc. [www.nadsa.com]

SPEECH LANGUAGE PATHOLOGIST

CLUSTER:

#8 Verbal

WHERE TO SURF:

- American Speech-Language-Hearing Association [www.professional.asha.org]
- American Academy of Audiology [www.audiology.org]

SPEECH THERAPY

CLUSTER:

#6 Human Services

WHERE TO SURF:

- American Speech-Language-Hearing Association [www.professional.asha.org]
- American Academy of Audiology [www.audiology.org]

SPORTS/ENTERTAINMENT

CLUSTER:

#10 Technical Arts

WHERE TO SURF:

- University of Massachusetts Sports Management Program [www.umass.edu]
- Street & Smith Sports Business Journal [www.sportsbusinessjournal.com]

STATISTICS

CLUSTER:

#2 Computational

WHERE TO SURF:

- American Statistical Association [www.amstat.org]
- American Mathematical Society [www.ams.org]

SURGICAL TECHNOLOGY

CLUSTER:

#4 Allied Health

WHERE TO SURF:

- Association of Surgical Technologists [www.ast.org]
- Liaison Council on Certification for the Surgical Technologist [www.icc-st.org]

TECHNICAL WRITING

CLUSTER:

#8 Verbal

WHERE TO SURF:

- Society for Technical Communication [www.stc.org]

TELECOMMUNICATIONS MANAGEMENT

CLUSTER:

#1 Applied Technology

WHERE TO SURF:

- International Brotherhood of Electrical Workers, Telecommunications Department [www.ibew.org]
- Communications Workers of America [www.cwa-union.org]
- Society of Cable and Telecommunications Engineers [www.scte.org]

THEATER

CLUSTER:

#9 Fine /Professional Art

WHERE TO SURF:

- National Association of Schools of Theater [www.nast.arts-accredit.org]
- Directors Guild of America [www.dga.org]
- Screen Actors Guild [www.sag.org]
- Producers Guild of America [www.producersguild.org]

THEOLOGY

CLUSTER:

#5 Social Sciences

WHERE TO SURF:

• The Association of Theological Schools [www.seekgod.ca/ats.htm]

TRAVEL

CLUSTER:

#6 Human Services

WHERE TO SURF:

• Career Exploration Center [www.utexas.edu/student/careercenter/careers/adventure.html]

URBAN PLANNING

CLUSTER:

#1 Applied Technology

WHERE TO SURF:

• American Planning Association, Education Division [www.planning.org]

URBAN STUDIES

CLUSTER:

#5 Social Sciences

WHERE TO SURF:

• The Urban Institute [www.urban.org]

• Urban History Association [www.unl.edu/uha/UHA.html]

VETERINARY SCIENCE

CLUSTER:

#3 Science-Related

WHERE TO SURF:

• American Veterinary Medical Association [www.avma.org]

• Association of American Veterinary Medical Colleges [www.aavmc.org]

VETERINARY TECHNOLOGY

CLUSTER:

#4 Allied Health

WHERE TO SURF:

- National Association of Veterinary Technicians in America [www.navta.net]
- Association of American Veterinary Medical Colleges [www.aavmc.org]

WEB DESIGN

CLUSTER:

#1 Applied Technology

#8 Verbal

#10 Technical Arts

WHERE TO SURF:

- Web Design and Developers Association [www.wdda.org]

WOMEN'S STUDIES

CLUSTER:

#5 Social Sciences

WHERE TO SURF:

- Artemis Guide to Women's Studies in the U.S. [www.artemisguide.com]

ZOOLOGY

CLUSTER:

#3 Science-Related

WHERE TO SURF:

- The American Zoo and Aquarium Association [www.aza.org]

College Planning Guides from Octameron

Don't Miss Out: The Ambitious Student's Guide to Financial Aid **$14.00**
Hailed as the top consumer guide to student aid, Don't Miss Out covers scholarships, loans, and personal finance strategies. It will save readers hundreds, if not thousands of dollars in college costs.

The A's and B's of Academic Scholarships **$14.00**
Money for being bright! This book describes 100,000 awards offered by nearly 1200 colleges. Best of all, most of these (which must be used at the sponsoring school) are not based on financial need.

Loans and Grants from Uncle Sam **$8.00**
Increase your eligibility for federal student aid. This guide describes it all—the aid application process as well as loans and grants for students, parents and health professionals.

Financial Aid FinAncer: Expert Answers to College Financing Questions **$8.00**
Learn how special family circumstances impact on student aid.

The Winning Edge: The Student-Athlete's Guide to College Sports **$9.00**
It's all here. Scholarship opportunities. NCAA rules and regulations. Advice from coaches. Sample athletic resumes. Strategies, timetables, and worksheets—all to help you take your sport to college!

Behind the Scenes: An Inside Look at the College Admission Process **$8.00**
Who get in, and why? Through question and answer sections and case studies, you can view the admission process from the inside. Originally written by Ed Wall, former Dean of Admission at Amherst College; updated by Janet Adams-Wall, Director of College Counseling at The Governor's Academy.

Do It Write: How to Prepare a Great College Application **$8.00**
Personalize your essays so they stand out from the crowd. Author Gary Ripple is the former Admission Director at Lafayette College and the College of William and Mary

College Match: A Blueprint for Choosing the Best School for You **$12.00**
Author Steve Antonoff combines dozens of easy-to-use worksheets with lots of practical advice to make sure you find schools that meet your needs and your preferences.

Campus Pursuit: Making the Most of the Visit and Interview **$7.00**
Nervous about your interview? In his companion book to Do-It Write, Gary Ripple gives advice to help you shine, as well as show you how to maximize the benefits of a campus visit.

College.edu: On-Line Resources for the Cyber-Savvy Student **$12.00**
Lost in Cyberspace? College.edu takes you to hundreds of useful sites on admission and financial aid, giving you Internet tips and warnings along the way.

Campus Daze: Easing the Transition from High School to College **$8.00**
Learn what to expect during your first year of college and how to succeed starting on Day One. Author George Gibbs is the former Dean of Admission and Freshmen at Muhlenberg College.

College Majors That Work **$10.00**
Get in. Get out. Get a job. Worksheets help match a student's goals and expectations with the right college major and explores how that choice plays out in the real world—influencing both career and lifestyle options. Written by Michael P. Viollt, President of Robert Morris College (IL).

Desk Set **$85.00**
One copy of each of the above publications.

Ordering Information

Send Orders to: Octameron Associates, PO Box 2748, Alexandria, VA 22301, or contact us at: 703-836-5480 (voice), 703-836-5650 (fax), octameron@aol.com (e-mail).

Order Online: www.octameron.com.

Postage and Handling: Please include $3.00 for one publication, $5.00 for two publications $6.00 for three publications and $7.00 for four or more publications (and for Desk Sets).

Method of Payment: Payment must accompany order. We accept checks, money orders, American Express, Visa and MasterCard. If ordering by credit card, please include the card number and its expiration date.